Talking about Concertos

ANTONY HOPKINS

Talking about

CONCERTOS

an analytical study of
a number of well-known concertos
from Mozart to the present day

WADSWORTH PUBLISHING COMPANY INC.

BELMONT, CALIFORNIA

© Antony Hopkins 1964

Printed in Great Britain

ILLUSTRATIONS

The diagrams and musical examples
have been drawn by Jonathan Barkwith.

TO WALTER TODDS, THE GENTLE CENSOR

CONTENTS

ONE AGAINST ALL

ALL MEN are not born equal; even in the somewhat limited field of musical executants, some are endowed with infinitely greater natural ability than others. Take a brother and sister from the same family, bring them up with the same opportunities, send them to the same teacher, ensure that they practise for exactly equal amounts and it makes no difference; at the end of ten years one will have outstripped the other, almost inevitably. The concerto as a musical form is a logical reflection of the fact that in any group of musicians gathered under one roof, one or two will outshine the others in technical and musical ability.

In the very early days, concertos tended to be for several players rather than one. There is a charming proof of why this was so in one of the Handel concerti grossi for strings; in such a work, a string quartet—in fact the leaders of each section of violins, violas and 'cellos—will have passages of greater complexity than will be given to the main body of string players. In the slow movement of the piece in question, there is a particularly elaborate ornament given to the solo quartet which at no time appears in the ordinary orchestral parts, for the simple reason that the rank-and-file players would have been unable to play it with the requisite neatness and agility. In other words, Handel had not conceived the form itself as something special; it was simply a composition for orchestra which reflected the superiority of the front-desk performers. Put yourself in the place of a composer like Haydn with a resident orchestra at his disposal in the Eszterházy household, or Bach, working with the local players at Cöthen or Leipzig. It would only have been common sense to acknowledge the fact that Herr X or Dr Y was the outstanding performer on the oboe or the violin; what more natural, then, than to write a work which showed off this greater ability? Thus the early concertos came about, and herein lies the explanation of the seemingly haphazard choice of instruments which composers so often appear to have made at the time.

The emergence of the soloist into the splendid isolation he came to occupy in the nineteenth century was a slow process. In the Bach concertos for violin or keyboard, the soloist usually plays with the orchestra at all times, establishing the tempo and generally acting as an orchestral 'leader'. Even in such a case as the slow movement of Bach's D minor keyboard concerto, where there is no indicated part for the right hand until the thirteenth bar, it seems certain that the harpsichordist would have played with the accompanying strings, perhaps directing them with an elegant wave of the right hand at times in order to show his complete command of the situation. Gradually the competence of orchestral players increased to such an extent that they could manage without the assistance of the soloist; remember though that the conductor as we know him today was still unknown in 1700. Reports tell us of such barbarous customs as the audible beating of time with a stick upon the floor, or with a roll of parchment on the lid of the harpsichord. Where direction was necessary it would almost invariably come from the keyboard player, but there seems to have been a remarkable absence of formality about musical proceedings, even in the complex world of opera. Johann Mattheson, who was not only a composer, harpsichordist, organist and singer, but a linguist, a dancer and skilled fencer as well, when singing a role in an opera, would periodically leave the stage and direct the music from the harpsichord in the pit. It was on 5 December 1704 that he found an obstinate young man called Handel at the keyboard who refused to give way, thereby provoking the challenge to a duel which is a well-authenticated incident in Handel's life. Honour was satisfied when Mattheson's foil, having easily penetrated Handel's guard, impaled itself on one of his waistcoat buttons. This story is not entirely irrelevant, since Handel was accustomed to delight audiences at the opera-house by performing his keyboard concertos as interval music.

It was Mozart who established what we now think of as the

classical concerto form. In essence what he did was to devise a grand sonata for soloist and orchestra, though there are certain differences between strict sonata form[1] and the normal pattern of a Mozart concerto. What is the normal pattern? It is hard to say, since nearly every work of this kind has points of originality which make it an exception to any presupposed set of rules. For what it is worth, though, here is a rough ground-plan.

An orchestral exposition[2] presents us with most of the salient themes; but whereas in a sonata exposition the second subject will be in the so-called dominant key (a fifth higher than the tonic or 'home' key), in a concerto it is very much more likely to be kept in the original tonality. To make things more confusing, the composer will sometimes refuse to reveal the true second subject at all at this stage, preferring to save it up as a special treat for the soloist. (Beethoven and Mozart both have a lovable habit of fobbing us off with a 'dummy' second subject which, having been hailed with shrill cries of delight by the musical analyst, then fails to reappear until the recapitulation, much to our discomfiture.) On the whole, modulation to remote keys is avoided in the early stages, as this too is that much more effective if kept in reserve for a later moment. What distinguishes good concerto material from purely symphonic music is a very subtle suggestion that something is missing; that the music so far, although beautiful and satisfying enough in itself, has implications of potential decoration in the future. As the simplest possible instance of this I will quote two bars from the exposition of Mozart's piano concerto in G, K.453. They first appear in this very stark guise, and I would like to underline the fact that their extreme simplicity should plant a seed of suspicion in our minds.

Ex. I

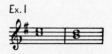

---

[1] For a detailed analysis of sonata form see Chapter I of *Talking about Symphonies*.

[2] Known as the *tutti*, from the Italian word for *everybody* - meaning that all instruments are playing.

When the equivalent moment is reached after the soloist's entry, we find this rudimentary phrase undergoing a delightful transformation. In the first place it is decorated with elegant syncopations:

and in the second with something even more elaborate:

Experience teaches us to recognize such moments and to await expectantly the pleasures that lie ahead. In other words, we should not regard the orchestral exposition as something cut off from the main part of the movement, but rather as the framework of a plot into whose events the hero (or soloist) will duly move as chief protagonist. All the same, this orchestral introduction, or *tutti* as it is usually called, will often finish with a formal conclusion, terminating in a polite silence before the soloist plays a note. As composers became more adept at handling the form, the solo instrument's entry was managed with increasing subtlety, as we shall discover in later chapters in this book.

Now it might be thought inevitable that the soloist should begin with the first subject as presented to us by the orchestra, and indeed there are plenty of Mozart concertos where that is what happens. But in four[1] out of the twenty-three works he wrote for piano and orchestra the soloist begins with completely new material, while in at least five others Mozart has devised some novel entry in which the orthodox presentation of the first subject is effectively disguised. In time, though, the soloist is bound to admit the existence

[1] K. 415, 466, 482, 491.

of the main theme; even so, it is by no means unusual to have it re-stated on the orchestra with the soloist merely adding decorative figures above. Perhaps the most original of all Mozart's variants on this very flexible plan occurs in the A major violin concerto, K.219. The soloist enters not only with a completely new theme, but at a totally different tempo as well. Then, the violin having discoursed most eloquently for a minute or so above a discreetly murmuring and pastoral accompaniment from the orchestra, the opening tempo is restored. Only at this point do we realize that the orchestral exposition, which had offered us what had seemed frankly to be one of Mozart's less inspired themes, was in fact merely an accompaniment, such as might be found at the beginning of an especially elaborate aria. It is the soloist who presents us with the true first subject, which is superimposed above the very same bars with which the orchestra had begun the work. Unorthodoxy can go no further.

Our search for a normal concerto form continues, however, and with the entry of the soloist we have reached what might be termed a secondary exposition. Exceptions there may be, but as a general principle composers at this point will re-state the opening material, this time including the soloist together with any additional comments he may care to make. In character this new statement is often much more akin to a development than an exposition, in that there is nothing to stop the composer journeying off into new episodes that have little or no relevance to what has gone before. One of the great excitements of concerto form is the element of fantasy it so often implies.

The line of demarcation between this secondary exposition and the development proper is a fine one, not always easy to perceive; all the same, there is a difference, and the introduction of new themes, excursions into more remote keys, even changes of tempo, are all more likely to occur in the true development section. Do not expect, however, such a concentration on the matter in hand as we find in the Mozart G minor symphony or Beethoven's fifth. In many concertos the development is an excuse for rhapsodic interludes; showers of notes may fly from the pianist's fingers, weaving delightful patterns that are in fact no more than decorative formulae of little thematic interest. If the themes are referred to, they are more likely to be found in the orchestral part, rather as though the orchestra was a crowd of anxious nannies trying to dissuade a capricious child from going too far on its own. Nevertheless, Mozart's greatest inspirations often occur in the development, and it is usually at the moment immediately *before* the recapitulation that we find those passages whose harmonic tension (and consequently emotional intensity) are the greatest.

The recapitulation, once reached, will certainly begin with a re-statement of the first subject, usually with a more co-operative attitude from the soloist than heretofore. But for the audience it is no time to sit back; the chance of new happenings at this point is far greater in a concerto than in a sonata or symphony. Not only is variety easier to achieve because of the contrast in colours between soloist and orchestra, but also there is always this element, already alluded to, of improvisation, of fantasy, which is an intrinsic part of the form. One thing we can be pretty sure of, though, is that at some point the soloist will drop out and allow the orchestra its head for a while. This convention is based on a purely practical reason in that it is designed to give the soloist a rest before he embarks on the most strenuous part of the movement, the cadenza.

The cadenza, rather despised by the purists, is for me one of the most fascinating attributes of the concerto. In the days of Bach, Mozart or Handel, and indeed right up to the time of Chopin or Liszt, the ability to improvise or make up music on the spur of the moment was expected from every musician. Matches were even held in which two performers would be sat down in turn at the keyboard and called upon to extemporize on a given theme. The cadenza gave an opportunity for the performer to display this skill, and while technical virtuosity was certainly called for, further development of the thematic material was as important. It is unlikely that truly improvised cadenzas were ever heard at public performances, since any sensible performer would presumably have prepared something in the process of learning the work. But the stimulus of an audience may well have provoked new flights of fancy, and most particularly the presence of other musicians in the surrounding orchestra would be likely to encourage the performer to new invention. What is undeniable is that the style of composition shown in those cadenzas by Mozart or Beethoven which have been written down is different from their usual manner. This is even true of the three-part keyboard fugue with which Bach's *Musical Offering* begins. It seems almost certain that this is a more or less exact transcription from memory of a piece that Bach had improvised on the spot to King Frederick. In it we find passages of free figuration that are quite un-fugal in character, as though Bach was doodling happily with his fingers while his brain was working out further possibilities of manipulating the fugue subject. Cadenzas, then, are the nearest thing we have to a recording of the great composers, for even if we make allowance for 'improvements' that may have crept in once the notes were put down on paper, it still seems likely that a cadenza by Bach, Mozart or Beethoven represents a reasonably honest transcription of what they would actually have improvised.

If the cadenza was a truly spontaneous invention, there had to be some indication to the orchestra that it was time they took up their instruments once again, and so it became established that a trill, or series of trills, was a signal to stand by. In due course the orchestra would enter with a triumphant affirmation of the first subject, whereupon (in nearly all of the Mozart concertos) the soloist would remain quiet till the end of the movement. It wasn't long before composers realized that the omission of the solo instrument from the final bars of a movement was a miscalculation, and Mozart himself, who thought of nearly everything—including serial music according to some wishful thinkers—experimented with the possibility of using the soloist right up to the end of a movement.[1]

The second movement of the classical concerto is designed to show the poetic and lyrical qualities of the instrument. It is often the movement which displays the deepest feeling, but it is misleading

[1] e.g. in K.491, the C minor concerto.

to expect this in all concertos, as sometimes the composer may prefer to write what is virtually a song without words, a movement whose function is decorative rather than contemplative. The early Mozart slow movements conform very much to the fashion of the times; they are elegant, elaborate in decoration, but relatively unadventurous in harmony. Even the melodies lack that truly personal distinction that he found in the last ten years of his life. Once the intensely romantic strain in his nature enabled him to overcome the artificialities and inhibitions of the musical language of his era, he was to write in his concertos some of the most profoundly expressive slow movements that have ever been conceived. As to the form of these movements, it is impossible to lay down any clear ruling. Some are variations, some are rondos, some are sonata movements. A typical example might begin with the solo piano playing the main theme; at its first appearance it will be relatively free from decoration and will as it were simply be offered to the orchestra, who will in their turn play it without comment from the soloist. A so-called 'episode' might follow in which soloist and orchestra will become more closely linked. Further discussion of the first theme could then lead to another more dramatic episode in which the soloist might well indulge in those wide melodic leaps which are so much a hallmark of Mozart's mature style. According to the length and complexity of the movement we could then either return to the opening material for the last time, or be led into new developments. Form in slow movements is of less importance than it is in an opening allegro; there must be a shape that is satisfying to the listener, but the form is not essential to the actual drama as it so often is in a sonata movement. It is usually sufficient for us to sit back and wonder at the beauty of the ideas that are presented to us; we do not need to be so aware of structures and relationships.

The third and last movement (four-movement concertos are a rarity) is most usually a rondo, a form in which one tune appears a number of times with varying 'fillings' between the repetitions—a multi-decker sandwich in which the rondo-theme is the bread, and the layers of cheese, salami and lettuce are the intervening episodes. Mozart also uses variation-form on occasions, and even a sonata movement is not unknown. Professor Girdlestone[1] has classified the one hundred and eleven finales of Mozart's maturity into seventy-six rondos, eighteen sonata-form movements and seventeen which are variations or minuets. Whatever the form, the function of the last movement is clearly to entertain; as in the symphony or the sonata, each movement serves a different purpose, the first to stimulate thought by elegant conversation about serious matters, the second to relax or edify, the third to delight and amuse. But there are exceptions to practically every statement that can be made about concertos, as of all large-scale musical forms it is the most flexible.

We come now to one of the most fascinating aspects of the growth of the piano concerto. If you want to buy a string instrument, and money is no object, you get one that is more than two hundred years old; there have been minor technical modifications to the violin, but basically it has remained unaltered. To buy a two-hundred-year-old piano with the intention of performing on it publicly would be the act of an unpractical eccentric; the instrument has changed out of all recognition and early examples are only really of interest to the antiquarian or the musicologist. The tone was dry and 'woody', it had little sustaining power, its compass was substantially less than that of the modern piano, its volume limited. The piano on which Mozart would have performed bore as little relationship to a modern concert grand as a 1900 Mercedes did to the sports racing car with which Stirling Moss won the Mille Miglia in 1955. This is a fact, but it is a fact from which we must draw the right conclusions. Mozart's scoring is wonderfully calculated in its balance between soloist and orchestra; whenever an important theme is given to the keyboard, the orchestra will either be silent or make sympathetic accompanying noises. On the other hand, many passages where the

---

[1] C. M. Girdlestone: *Mozart's Piano Concertos* (Cassell).

melodic interest lies in the woodwind or strings may be embellished by decorative cascades or notes from the piano, since there was no likelihood of their being obscured. It is these passages that are most liable to be distorted in modern performances; the dazzling technique and prodigious tone of the concert pianist of today causes figures which Mozart clearly intended to be no more than a silver lining to swamp the orchestra. This is especially true in all too many gramophone recordings, where the already disturbed balance is made still more remote from Mozart's conception by artificial means. There is no need to deny ourselves the virtues of the modern piano when it comes to subtlety of touch, beauty of tone and sustaining power. But we must scale down its resources in sheer volume and brilliance, or we will get a totally false impression of the actual musical content of a Mozart concerto.

In his first three piano concertos it is fairly clear that Beethoven had exactly the same problem to deal with as had Mozart. He rigs the balance in just the same way, never allowing the piano to compete openly with the orchestra. In the fourth concerto, which is the last truly classical concerto[1], the implied contest between soloist and orchestra is won by gentleness; this is most notably true of the slow movement in which the aggression of the orchestra is marvellously tamed by a constant turning of the other cheek, a refusal to fight which ultimately reduces the opponent to silence. Between the composition of his fourth and fifth piano concertos Beethoven apparently came into possession of a new piano. Despite his deafness he at once realized the potentialities of the instrument, and in the so-called 'Emperor' we see the result of his re-assessment of the relationship between piano and orchestra. Here for the first time in musical history the piano stands up to the orchestra as an equal, even indulging in open defiance at times. (For a detailed discussion of this work see Chapter VI.)

The last half of the nineteenth century saw a continuous increase in the demands that composers and pianists made upon the instrument, and in all fairness one must acknowledge the efforts of piano manufacturers to meet those demands. Improvements of

[1] until Stravinsky!

one kind or another were constantly being made and even in recent years new refinements have been invented. A small price has been paid for the enormously improved quality of sound, for the modern keyboard does have a deeper touch than Mozart would ever have known, which means that more energy is needed in the quicker-moving passages. The aesthetic problems raised by the changes in the instrument remain some of the most eternally fascinating in music, and every performer must come to terms with his own conscience in deciding how to play the classical repertoire.

The popular appeal of the concerto, and the piano concerto in particular, is enormous. The reason for this is fairly obvious. To be a hero one must vanquish an outnumbering opposition. In the public eye, the soloist is a sort of hero, dominating the orchestra, and triumphing despite tremendous odds. An element of self-projection enters in, and the listener gets a vicarious thrill by imagining himself to be in the soloist's place. (Did he realize one tenth of the work entailed in achieving the standard of performance which any concerto demands, he might think twice about it.) To the soloist, the concerto remains the ultimate challenge. There is little logic in this, since to play a solo sonata of the dimensions of the Hammerklavier or the Liszt B minor would seem to be even more demanding. In the long run, it must be this very situation of 'one against all' that makes the concerto what it is, for every story needs a hero with whom the reader can identify himself. The hero in a concerto is just that much more obvious. . . .

CHAPTER II

MOZART

Piano Concerto in D minor, K.466 (1785)

1. Allegro. 2. Romance. 3. Rondo: prestissimo.

Orchestra: 1 flute; 2 oboes; 2 bassoons; 2 horns; 2 trumpets; 2 timpani; strings.

BEFORE we begin to explore this work in any detail it might be helpful to think about the language of music and the way in which a composer of Mozart's stature uses its vocabulary. For the moment let us confine ourselves to the familiar but sometimes arduous process of learning a language that is foreign to us. The grown-up normally goes through a fairly agonizing period of '*Avez-vous un' chambre avec deux lits pour ce nuit*—or should it be *cette nuit?*—Oh dear, it is so difficult.' The receptionist then says in perfect English, 'Sorry sir, the hotel is full', and you try again elsewhere. The child, on the other hand, absorbs a language without much difficulty, but seldom has an adult perception of its ultimate possibilities. He may have Corneille and Racine crammed into his head at school and be profoundly bored by them, whereas later in life he may regret not having learnt enough French to be able to appreciate them properly. Now it is my belief that a true appreciation of music can only come with a deep understanding of its language, and there is no better illustration of the need to develop a really discriminating ear than the opening of this concerto. All musicians accept that it is one of the great works; they also realize that its greatness lies partly in its unusually romantic and turbulent quality. Yet if we reduce its opening phrases to their bare bones it would seem to be pretty trivial stuff, for this is the framework on which it is built:

Ex. 4

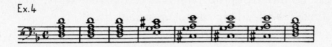

Now it is undeniable that that is pretty poverty-stricken as music, and it is equally undeniable that a great composer can use such a framework and construct a masterpiece upon it. How? Let us return once again to the analogy of language.

Pick a few simple words and throw them into a hat. As nouns we will select 'sun, winter, home, wages, task, heat'; as verbs let us have 'fear, do, go, take, have'. All simple words. Throw in a few make-weights like 'no, the, more' and so on and we still have nothing that is not in common use. Even if we add 'worldly' or 'furious' we are scarcely plunging into the extremes of rhetoric. Let us now make a sentence from these simple components.

'Furious at the winter, I've gone from home to get some sun and heat. I'll take my wages—no more worldly tasks for me.'

As prose, this is grisly, but I have simply tried to assemble the given words into some sort of order, just as the anguished tourist does with his 'Avez-vous un' chambre avec deux lits pour ce nuit'. But what can those same words do in the hands of a master?

> Fear no more the heat o' the sun
> Nor the furious winter's rages;
> Thou thy worldly task hast done,
> Home art gone and ta'en thy wages.

What wonderful stuff it is; and yet the words in themselves are so very ordinary. Now can we improve on Shakespeare? Suppose that instead of 'Fear no more the heat o' the sun' we say, 'The intensity of temperature from the solar system will no longer harm you.' The thought may be the same but the poetry has vanished. It is not the thought, then, that makes the line poetic but the way in which the thought is expressed. With this in mind let us return to Ex. 4. In itself this sequence of chords has little value, but it can be dressed up in a number of different ways. You could decorate it with a long sustained melody:

Or you could turn it into a stately sarabande:

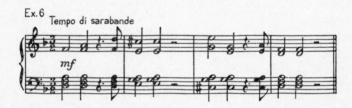

Equally well it can be made heroic, though I will admit that this version smacks a little of amateur theatricals:

This is no more remarkable than it would be to suggest a simple idea such as sunset to three different poets. One might express himself in these words:

> The sun descending in the west,
> The evening star does shine;
> The birds are silent in their nest,
> And I must seek for mine.

Another would choose a different way of expressing the same thought:

> The day's grown old, the fainting sun
> Has but a little way to run;
> And yet his steeds, with all his skill
> Scarce lug the chariot down the hill.

And a third, in a more sombre mood, might say:

> The curfew tolls the knell of parting day,
> The lowing herd wind slowly o'er the lea,
> The plowman homeward plods his weary way,
> And leaves the world to darkness and to me.

The basic idea is the same in all three verses, but the words in each case are different. There is, however, a greater difference, one that can only be appreciated after we become interested in words for their own sake rather than in the thoughts which they are used to express.

Now if, as I have suggested, the effect of a poem depends not just on its meaning as a statement of fact or a description of events, nor even on any intrinsic quality in the words chosen, such as 'fear, heat, sun, west, star, etc.', the clue to its quality must lie more in the order of words and their relationship to each other. The word 'chimney-sweeper' has no great merit; but a genius like Shakespeare will put it in the very next line to a lyrical phrase such as 'Golden lads and girls'—

> Golden lads and girls all must,
> As chimney-sweepers, come to dust.

The bright sunlight in the word 'golden' is, so to speak, cancelled out, blackened by the associations of soot and chimney and the dark enclosing tunnel above the dead ash of the fire. If we appreciate these things we are appreciating the subtlety of the poet's use of language, not just accepting the statement at its face-value. The same thing applies to music; listening to the opening *tutti* of a concerto such as this, we need to take into consideration far more than just the fact that to start with it consists of simple alternations between the chords of D minor and the dominant seventh in A.[1] Here now is Mozart's version of Ex. 4:

Ex.8 Allegro

In order to appreciate this fully we need to be well enough read in music to be able to compare it with a host of other works. First we need to relate it to Mozart's twenty-two other concertos for piano and orchestra—not necessarily knowing them all in detail, but being aware of their individual qualities, whether lyrical, dramatic, spring-like, immature or tragic. Not one of them begins with this sort of muttering uneasiness, nor with these restless syncopations. This alone, then, should be enough to make us listen with special attention. Next we need to know enough about Mozart's style to realize the significance of this type of figure in the bass.

Ex. 9

[1] The proper term for the chord in bar 4 of Ex. 4.

In his terms, such a figure is not just an empty gesture; rather will it imply a certain dramatic force, and when it is in a minor key, as it is here, there will inevitably be a suggestion of considerable agitation.

If we cast the net a little wider and take in the whole of the opening orchestral chapter, another unusual aspect of the music should strike us. I doubt if there is a single introductory *tutti* in all the Mozart concertos that stays so single-mindedly in the same mood for such a long time as this. It has a length of aim, a fixity of purpose that is remarkable. This is partly because of his refusal to pamper us with a really substantial melody. He constantly leads us to believe that one is going to appear, but all the time the music is driven forward with these uneasy syncopations; never does he allow it to settle. Lastly we should bear in mind the matter of key and all that goes with the implications of D minor in Mozart's world.

This is what I mean by an appreciation of music. Now one has to admit, however reluctantly, that many people in their endeavour to grapple with the language of music never get beyond the 'Avez-vous un' chambre' stage. To them the language will always remain unfamiliar, and the sheer lack of vocabulary will limit their horizon enormously. There are others who press on to the stage of being able to translate reasonably fluently; they can even at times 'think' in the language. But the ultimate appreciation of a concerto such as this demands a complete receptivity to Mozart's thought, so that the placing of every note in its context becomes significant. The proverbial man-in-the-street *can* enjoy this as a fairly typical classical concerto with rattling runs on the piano and a nice tune popping up now and then. This is because the superficial aspects of Mozart's language are now very familiar to us; all the more reason, then, that it should take a particularly perceptive ear to re-assess the striking originality of Mozart's ideas. Enough of preliminary thoughts: let us turn to the work itself.

As we have already discovered, there is an unusual consistency of mood in the opening *tutti*. So often Mozart alternates between a positive heroic statement and a gentle reply; here the music stays turbulent for the first thirty-two bars. There is a moment's silence and then we are introduced to the second subject:

Cast as it is in the form of question and answer, this is ideal concerto material, and it is no surprise that when it reappears it is divided between orchestra and piano. For the moment it is enough that it eases the tension so far generated by the music; what we do not realize at this time is that there is another whole paragraph to this tune that Mozart still keeps hidden from us. It seems too early for this second subject really to establish itself and it is soon swept aside by a new and stormy phrase. With a dramatic intensity that we tend to associate more with Beethoven than Mozart the music drives remorselessly on. Only in the few bars immediately before the soloist's entry do we find any further traces of tenderness, and even here the theme is of such a pathetic character that it does little to soften the impression of a soul in torment that has been so clearly conveyed. And now, at the critical point of the solo entry, what does Mozart have in store for us? Not as might be expected a reflection of the dark uneasiness of the preceding pages, nor even a conventionally heroic gesture such as a scale or arpeggio. In a meltingly beautiful phrase he offers us at least some feeling of comfort, though there is obviously still an element of sadness involved.

This theme is to be the exclusive property of the soloist; at no point of the movement does any member of the orchestra even touch on it. It isn't long, though, before the soloist finds himself very much involved with the orchestra. The strings begin the disturbed rhythms of Ex. 8 once again (the secondary exposition), this time with reinforcement from the piano. The harmonies are strikingly dissonant in Mozart's subtle way, much use being made of sevenths and seconds.

Ex.12

Important though the piano part is, it is the orchestral music that contains the heart of the matter here; the piano figuration merely adds an extra bite to the harmony.

In due course Ex. 10 reappears, this time divided attractively between orchestra and soloist, until we shortly meet the second part of the second subject, an elegant and graceful tune that was well worth waiting for.

Ex.13

This is seized on with delight by the orchestra while the soloist decorates it further with descending scales that are not a bit less delightful for being a convention of the period. For a short time it even seems as though the thundery mood of the opening has been entirely forgotten. But it is not to be; gradually the piano writing becomes more jagged in outline, leading us back inevitably to another section for orchestra alone in which the music of the first pages appears once more. Some of the brooding intensity is dispelled however by the fact that it is now in F major instead of D minor.

We have now met all the main themes of the movement and from here on the interest lies in their changing relationships. One cannot say what the music *means* precisely. We are aware of many fluctuations of mood, of moments of extreme tension, of other periods of relative calm; but it is part of the mystery of music that it can play on our emotions without there being any rational justification for change. It is enough that our response should mirror in detail every subtle nuance of feeling that the music contains, remembering at all times that this is not cold, detached or conventional in its classical perfection, but Mozart at his most romantic and impassioned. The mood remains disturbed right up to the end of the movement, the orchestra having an unusually lengthy concluding chapter (or coda) which in no way lessens the perturbation of spirit that the music has so signally conveyed.

From this dark unease there now emerges a phrase that combines both innocence and beauty. Mozart calls this second movement a Romance, a term to which too much significance should not be attached, as it was in quite common usage at the time. But partly because of its context it seems to have a special quality of sweetness even by Mozart's standards. The melody has two stanzas, each of which is played first by the soloist and then repeated by the orchestra. It is hard to imagine anything more eloquently civilized than this.

Ex. 14

Incidentally it is worth remarking that most performers today are so hypnotized by the word Romance that they probably take this movement far slower than Mozart intended. The time-signature is ₵, which means *alla breve* or two-in-a-bar; we usually hear it as a rather slow four.

Now it makes little difference to Mozart whether he is writing a concerto for piano, violin, clarinet or what; his inspiration always conjures up what is essentially a vocal line translated into instrumental terms. The third piano entry in this movement introduces what is virtually an aria for piano which at a slightly lower pitch could easily be mistaken for one of those marvellous soprano parts that so delight us in operas like *Cosi Fan Tutte* or *Il Seraglio*. The left-hand part is perfunctory in the extreme; all the performer's attention must be concentrated on the difficult task of making the keyboard sing. Meanwhile the orchestra has a supporting accompaniment of apparent simplicity which all the same is full of subtlety. A limpid and effortless return to Ex. 14 concludes this lyrical chapter.

There follows the big surprise of the movement, a stormy middle section which now appears most unexpectedly, disrupting the calm beauty of what has gone before. It is as though the anxiety of the first movement has not after all been forgotten; here it casts its dramatic shadow over the second movement. Mozart gives no indication of a change of tempo, so here is confirmation that a fairly quick pace is justified in the first part. To play a passage of this type slowly is to deny its very nature; one would as soon cry 'Once more unto the breach, dear friends' in tones of milk and honey, for here is Mozart the virtuoso pianist as well as Mozart the composer.

Ex.15

col 8va bassa

The return to the former calm is wonderfully accomplished, with the soloist gradually easing the pace by a smooth transition through groups of six notes, then four, then three and lastly two to each crotchet beat. The opening tune is re-stated in full, this time with the pianist playing the whole span of the melody without the participation of the orchestra. Together they combine in a long coda in which new and tender themes ease away the last traces of tension.

The finale scarcely represents the joy unconfined we might reasonably expect. Mozart begins with the piano, and at once we are impressed with the urgency of the mood. Quick the tempo may be, but it is anything but cheerful.

Ex. 16

* Mozart also puts a C♮ here with great effect.

The orchestra is quite willing to follow this lead; in a matter of seconds the strings embark on a passage that is every bit as disturbed as anything from the first movement. The syncopations now are even more restless and the tension is if anything increased as one dissonance follows another. Comes the soloist's entry and once again Mozart catches us off our guard. Just as he did in the first movement he introduces a totally new theme. From a structural point of view this is no great surprise; it is the emotional character of the music that is unexpected.

Ex. 17

* The discrepancy of notation between right and left hands seems to be one of Mozart's rare errors—a slip of the pen, no doubt.

It is only a moment, however, before this new theme is rejected and swept aside by a fresh outburst of Ex. 16. An episode in F minor does nothing to reduce the tension, but then at last the sun seems to come out and in the twinkling of an eye Mozart transports us to a different world, a world where care is forgotten and gaiety can at last reign supreme. Surprisingly it is the orchestra that first leads us to this enchanted land.

Ex.18

The soloist endorses this change of heart, but even a tune as beguiling as this is destined to be soured by the prevailing mood. When this same happy theme reappears once more, it is in the minor, and much of its original character has been lost. Not until after a cadenza (which should obviously sustain the generally turbulent mood) is the deadlock ultimately broken. The key-signature of D major heralds a release from tension and Ex. 18 reappears in its happiest guise. In the last few pages a genuine gaiety is at last established convincingly, and the work ends in an atmosphere of radiant optimism.

What an extraordinary piece it is though for 1785. None of the Beethoven concertos betrays so disturbed a frame of mind, not even the third; as for the works of a still later period, they reflect a different concept of concerto-writing in which the piano part tends to ride roughshod over the orchestra, dominating by brute force where necessary and hogging the limelight most of the time. How can they be expected to rival the profound subtlety of this music, which expresses a state of emotional turmoil that makes it singularly apposite to our times? If only we can penetrate beyond the superficial familiarity of Mozart's idiom we will soon realize how intense and personal the message of this work is. When we do understand the language well enough to perceive its meaning, we shall be moved almost beyond bearing.

c

CHAPTER III

MOZART

Piano Concerto in A major, K.488 (1786)

1. Allegro. 2. Adagio. 3. Allegro assai.

Orchestra: 1 flute; 2 clarinets; 2 horns; 2 bassoons; strings.

IF THE CONCERTO in D minor discussed in the previous chapter can be said to show Mozart at his most romantic and impassioned, then this concerto is certainly the most lyrical. It is one of the supremely lovable works and is such an undiluted pleasure to listen to that there is even a danger that we may take it for granted. Has it not always been there, we feel, like summer skies, flowers, fountains and waterfalls? In many ways it is far less adventurous than the other concertos that are its immediate neighbours; it could well be described as the textbook example of the classical concerto except perhaps for its avoidance of virtuosity. Much of it lies within the technical grasp of a musically gifted child of twelve or thirteen, yet despite these handicaps, if handicaps they be, it remains for many people the loveliest of all his piano concertos. Partly this is because the tunes in which it abounds are themselves so beguiling.

These are presented in considerable detail in the long orchestral introduction with which the concerto begins. Nor, as is so often the case in Mozart's mature works for a solo instrument and orchestra, are these proffered riches to be ignored by the soloist; in due course he will welcome them all. Only three themes of real significance are kept in reserve for later in the movement, and each one of these when it does reappear is stated first by the orchestra. Mozart seems deliberately to have abstained from his favourite trick of holding back some especially delicious morsel for the soloist, as though to show a new originality by being entirely orthodox.

The mood of the work, which perfectly evokes that peculiarly Mozartian feeling that I have described elsewhere as 'tears behind the smile', is established by one crucial harmony in the very first bar. Imagine for the moment that Mozart had written this:

Ex.19

It's all quite smooth and effortless; the tune is undeniably pretty but it hasn't a great deal of character. Let us turn now to Mozart's own version and see what differences there may be.

Ex.20

The subtle poignancy of the G natural in bar 1 is a masterstroke, as is the clash between G sharp and A in the 4th beat of bar 2, and the less obvious dissonance between the chord of A major and the D in the bass in bar 4. It is these moments of harmonic tension that prevent the music from being merely bland; behind the sunny façade there are shadowy places.

For the first eighteen bars there is nothing of great importance apart from this vital tune; anything else is merely an offshoot from the main stem—what a gardener once described to me as 'unnatural growth', whatever that may mean. In the 18th bar we find an important episode, a passage which the orchestra is going to have several times even although the soloist only decorates it— and then by implication rather than direct statement. This passage too is deeply affected by the G natural we first experienced in bar 1.

Ex.21

This may appear to be drawn towards D major fairly positively, but it is in fact merely a flirtation, and G sharps in the very next bar restore the momentarily forsaken tonality of A.[1] It is this very ambiguity that makes the music so curiously emotional; the G natural preserves its character of a flattened seventh (which jazz musicians would call a 'blue' note) rather than seeming merely to be the fourth note in the scale of D.

As the music enters its 31st bar, the graceful second subject makes its appearance. Its general air of elegance is again prevented from sounding superficial by the occasional chromatic note and the subtle placing of a dissonance of sorts on the first beat of every bar.

Ex.22

Two more themes are worth quoting, both of which have suggestions of question and answer in them that lead us to suppose (rightly) that they will later be treated as a dialogue between piano and orchestra.

[1] For an extensive discussion of the importance of tonality in classical music see Chapter I of *Talking about Symphonies*.

All of these ideas are important, all are due to appear in decorated versions once the soloist has entered the scene. The 66-bar introduction ends with a firm no-nonsense cadence in A major and the piano part begins. Not here the capricious opening of concertos such as the ones in C minor, D minor or E♭ major, in which the soloist denies all knowledge of what has gone before, preferring to state his own material in his own terms. This is a work in which the sense of partnership between solo piano and orchestra is complete[1]; consequently it is with a feeling of welcoming back a dearly loved companion that we renew our acquaintance with Ex. 20, now presented to us in terms of such utter simplicity as to cause composers of later and more complex periods to despair. A few decorative runs of no great difficulty lead us onward to Ex. 21, which is first stated by the orchestra and then delightfully embellished by the soloist. Since the relationship may seem obscure to the uninitiated ear I will clarify it by this little three-part exercise in which the outer parts represent the solo pianist's

[1] In this respect it is interesting to note that in this concerto Mozart retained the old tradition of indicating that the soloist should play *with* the orchestra throughout the *tutti* as a means of holding the work together—a custom discontinued nowadays, of course.

contribution, and the middle line shows the implied reference to
Ex. 21.

Ex. 25

This passage is rounded off a little more dramatically, but it is
worth remarking the skill with which Mozart allows the frail tones
of his fortepiano to penetrate the orchestral texture. For the most
part, rests divide each chord on the wind from its next-door
neighbour, and in these fractional silences the silvery clatter of
leather hammer against string could have been clearly heard.

Ex. 22 now reappears, this time on solo piano and in the expected
'dominant' key of E major. For a few bars the orchestra sit back
and listen before taking over the melody in their turn, at which
point the piano obligingly decorates bars 2 and 4 of the melody
with a shimmering outline of broken octaves. Nothing could more
tellingly illustrate the balance between piano and orchestra that
Mozart had in mind than this passage, for each party in the conversation must listen to the other. Mutual support or embellish-
ment is perfectly acceptable, a stand-up argument is not.

Episodes based upon Exx. 23 and 24 now add a slightly disturbed
air to the music; the mood of sweetness engendered by the second
subject is momentarily threatened. Some more robust scale passages
bring about a change of heart, though, and a firm cadence in the key
of E leads us to a strong orchestral statement of Ex. 21. This dissolves
not into the decorative frills of Ex. 25 but into a moment's silence
from which emerges an entirely new theme, the first of the three
which have already been mentioned as not appearing in the
initial *tutti*.

Ex.26

At once the soloist seizes on this, decking it out in the prettiest imaginable two-part counterpoint. Now so far the mood of the movement has been almost entirely free from the dark and brooding style that Mozart increasingly adopted at this period of his life. But here shadows begin to fall—not dramatic ones, but vague intimations of disquiet. The music flirts with minor keys; wide-spaced intervals abound and the musical interest lies increasingly with the orchestra. The frail voice of the fortepiano hadn't sufficient weight to discuss these more serious matters; for the time being it is reduced entirely to decoration. It is at this point that the remaining two themes that have been withheld are introduced.

Ex.27ᵃ   Ex.27ᵇ

It will be seen that these two ideas are closely related in rhythm although different in contour and scoring. Both add more than a touch of poignancy to the proceedings and it takes a fairly lengthy bit of passage-work from the soloist to drag us out of the shadows and lead us once more to the lyrical first theme.

This, once reached, brings us to a remarkably orthodox re-capitulation where Mozart conspicuously avoids the dramatic surprises which abound in the more stormy concertos in the minor keys. The cadenza most frequently played is by Mozart himself, but I suspect that it was dashed off in a hurry for a pupil, since it is by no means his best. Compared to his magnificent cadenza for the concerto in G major, K.453, it is a shallow thing, having little in the way of new thematic development. A formal close by the orchestra duly rounds off the movement and we who know the concerto sit expectantly awaiting the sublime adagio which lies ahead.

This, one of the most perfect movements that even Mozart ever wrote, begins with the solo piano playing a melody whose opening phrase, once heard, can never be forgotten.[1]

Ex.28   Adagio

Deceptively simple to look at, it demands such subtlety of touch and phrasing that pianists can go on practising it all their lives. One of the hardest things is to connect up the low E sharp in bar 2. It is really part of the melodic line; great swoops of this type are very characteristic of Mozart's vocal writing, and this particular example shows clearly the way in which he regarded the keyboard as a sort of extension of the voice. Twelve bars of this melody lead us to the first orchestral entry. Orchestra and piano in this movement are like brother and sister, alike and yet different. The orchestra never plays the long melody that the piano has stated with such tenderness and melancholy, preferring its own material which in fact is equally beautiful. The texture is full of gentle dissonances and that imitative elegance that is the hallmark of the born contrapuntist.

[1] It is the only occasion that Mozart ever used the key of F♯ minor.

Ex.29

Everything follows on with what seems like an inevitable logic even although the next piano entry introduces yet another theme. For five bars the solo piano holds the stage alone; then we arrive at a moment of melting beauty as the music turns positively towards a major key for the first time in the movement. This significant change is marked by a hushed chord in the strings; it is not quite powerful enough to shake off the wistful quality that has so far prevailed, and we find ourselves in a sort of limbo half-way between A minor and A major. It is the orchestra that resolves the dilemma, opting firmly for A major with yet another theme given out by the woodwind.[1]

Ex.30

At last piano and orchestra agree that here is a tune worthy of their united attention, and for the first time in the movement we find a theme shared. It continues, decorated with languorous scales that are like the sighs and flutterings of the heroine of a Restoration comedy. The first theme returns, bringing the same response as before from the orchestra; but whereas the piano had formerly disregarded Ex. 29, this time it extends its strains still further with touching little embellishments that add to its emotional intensity. The coda was only sketched in by Mozart. Time after time one hears performers solemnly plonking their way through a line of

[1] Also used by Mozart in *Don Giovanni*.

single notes that would have been unthinkable to the composer. Since he was usually writing for himself, Mozart often resorted to a sort of shorthand in which he indicated the extreme outer notes of the phrases and no more.[1] All that is left for us at this point is this threadbare sketch.

Ex. 31

To Mozart, a literal performance of this would have seemed an abomination, for the simple reason that it would have sounded atrocious on the piano of his time. Gradually we are finding the courage to add some small elaboration to passages such as this, but usually we are so terrified of altering the text that we tend to drift into triviality. For what it is worth my instinct tells me that we are far too conservative in these matters. I suspect that a performer of Mozart's day would probably have done something more on these lines.

Ex. 32

If Mozart had wanted *less* than this it would have been no trouble for him to write it out—as he did in the subsequent bars. It is precisely because he was anticipating a fair number of notes to a bar that he resorted to shorthand at this point.

[1] There is a notable instance in the finale of the concerto in E♭, K.482.

The movement ends with as sad and tender a leave-taking as parting lovers ever lingered over, a last memory of Ex. 29 which the piano caresses with delicately repeated C sharps.

The final Rondo is sheer joy. The soloist sets the mood with its opening bars.

The orchestra takes up the idea with enthusiasm and embarks on an unusually long *tutti* in which the music stays resolutely in the key of A major without for a moment producing a sense of monotony. One theme in particular stands out as a sort of Instant Gavotte, galvanized at this tempo into new and unimagined activity.

The general air of high spirits is unmistakable. Delightful though it all is, it fails to capture the interest of the soloist, who has ideas of his own. Theme after theme flies from the keyboard in a positive burble of notes. The orchestra can hardly get a chord in edgeways, though at one point they do introduce a new theme.

At once the soloist seizes on it, decorating it with chromatic runs and using the C naturals in the sixth bar as a pivot to open the fairly remote door of C major. There is a brief excursion into foreign territory and then a swift and convincing return to E major, the most closely related key to the 'home' key of A. The chatter continues, the piano part seeming like a veritable *moto perpetuo*. One more theme must be mentioned before we finish our exploration of this totally enchanting work. It is like a children's game of going upstairs and down again. No more than a scale really, it wears an air of being something more important, an air that is completely spurious since its importance is that of a child wearing a grown-up hat.

Ex. 36

etc.

The flute is very drawn to this tune and proceeds to play with it in his own time, regardless of the fact that the piano has gone on to other things. To list every tune in the movement would make this a very long and unnecessarily arduous chapter. Mozart was never more generous in melody than he was in this concerto and it is hard to believe that he only had five years to live when he wrote it. It was a time when his inspiration was in full flood. Work after work poured from his pen, and nearly every one a masterpiece. Their craftsmanship and facility have never been surpassed, but as I warned earlier, let us not take such things for granted. Music like this is not common or everyday; if angels dance, this would serve them well.

CHAPTER IV

BEETHOVEN

Piano Concerto No. 2 in B♭ major, Op. 19 (1795)

1. Allegro con brio. 2. Adagio. 3. Rondo: molto allegro.

Orchestra: 1 flute; 2 oboes; 2 bassoons; 2 horns; strings.

THE FIRST VENTURE into a major musical form is something of an occasion for a composer, particularly if he is young and inexperienced. It may even inspire a certain reluctance—Brahms's refusal to commit himself to a symphony till after he was forty is a well-known example of this. In 1795 a young man called Beethoven, then aged twenty-four, was asked to play at a concert for the benefit of the widows and orphans of the Society of Musicians in Vienna. This was a big opportunity, and he was fired to compose a piano concerto for the occasion. As is so often the case, insufficient time had been allowed for him to write a major work, and with only two days to go the finale still hadn't been written. At this point, the poor young man had a nasty attack of colic. However, 'the show must go on' seems to have been an understood principle even in 1795, and poor Beethoven pressed on with the last movement with a doctor by his side, and four copyists in the next room; as each sheet of manuscript paper was completed by the suffering composer it was passed through the door and the desperate process of making a set of orchestral parts was continued.

When it came to the rehearsal another problem presented itself—the piano was half a tone flat. Despite the exhaustion that Beethoven must have felt after two frenzied days of composition, not to mention the aftermath of the colic, he rose manfully to the occasion and rehearsed the entire work, transposing it up a semi-tone into B major. As a feat of musicianship this seems all the more remarkable when we remember that he could have had no time to practise the notes properly and get them under his fingers. He must have been virtually sight-reading as well as transposing. Under the circumstances it is small wonder that the concerto got pushed aside and forgotten; Beethoven probably felt that it had somewhat sour memories for him. Three years later he revised it and issued it as his second, another one having been written in the interim. Ever since, there has been confusion in people's minds, since the concerto we know as No. 1 was actually written second and vice versa. Unfortunately I am not in a position to be able to compare the two versions—in fact I don't know if anyone can, as the original part was probably destroyed. But if the last movement stands more or less as it was when he wrote it, it must be the most entertaining work ever written by a man suffering from colic.

Now this concerto demonstrates admirably the need for the listener to have the widest possible receptivity to music. Composers obviously don't want us to listen to everything in the same mood; and since emotions can change far more rapidly in music then they ever would in a play, we must react more quickly than would the audience in a theatre. There is more to this than merely responding to the prevailing mood; if we look on the different movements as the acts of a play it requires no great critical faculty to be able to say that this act is dramatic, this sentimental and the other comical. We need to go a long way beyond that; for just as when we listen to Shakespeare we appreciate the beauty of language, the subtle inter-relationship of word and phrase, even while we laugh at the antics of Sir Toby and Sir Andrew, so in music we must learn to see in what *terms* a particular passage is dramatic, intense, tender, humorous, ironic, pathetic, or whatever.

In the first movement of this concerto we find an astonishingly rapid alternation of different emotions. The first bar is heroic:

Ex. 37

the next three, tender:

Ex. 38

Bar 5 takes us back to the heroic theme again, followed once more by a tender reply to balance the first. A pattern has been suggested—heroic-tender-heroic-tender, and so you, nice, responsive and intelligent listener that you are, expect a renewal of the heroic mood to conform to the pattern. Instead of complying with the suggested laws of symmetry, Beethoven introduces a melting new theme, all the more touching in that you should be expecting a reversion to the heroic mood at this point.

Ex. 39

A brief extension of this phrase leads us back to Ex. 37; but now what was openly heroic has become taut and nervous. The same pattern has been so translated by a change of orchestration as to produce an entirely different emotional reaction. One could perhaps make a reasonably convincing comparison between music and the theatre by saying that if this theme is our hero, the various versions of it that Beethoven produces show him in different situations which call for different behaviour on his part. Here, he would appear to be in some danger:

Where such comparisons come unstuck is that music is not governed by the logic of action, nor by a plot. What we have to do is to learn to respond in just as receptive a way as we do to a dramatic stimulus in the theatre, but without trying to translate music into the terms of a materialistic world. I regard it as entirely legitimate to say that a passage in music *resembles* a small boy cocking a snook at his elders; but I would regard it as a monstrous misinterpretation to suggest that the composer was actually describing such regrettable behaviour, unless he had given us his specific authority so to do.

That music is a language of a sort cannot seriously be doubted, for it communicates emotion and thought from one human being to another, which is about as good a definition of the function of language as you would arrive at after consultation with a hundred philosophers. Moreover, it is a language which deals largely in emotions, owing to the simple and inescapable fact that sound evokes an emotional response. A quiet sound is a sedative, a loud one is a stimulus; the same obviously applies to slow-moving or quick-moving music. Without becoming too obscure, one could say that the language of music deals with generalizations in a detailed and particular way. Ex. 37 shows us a generalized conception of the heroic, clad in classical dress. Beethoven, having once stated it, will discuss it in great detail, constantly changing our ideas as to its content and purpose. In addition to this he will concern himself with purely musical considerations such as modulation, rhythmic extension, decoration and so on. These in their turn may be said to have certain spiritual implications—the sense of remoteness conveyed by a modulation to a distant key for instance. In the long run then it is impossible to isolate one side of music from the other; its intellectual qualities may very well be the deepest source of its emotional impact. Lovers of Bach will know precisely what I mean. But let us return to the orchestral exposition of Beethoven's Op. 19.

After some fairly stormy excursions into other keys and some eloquent consideration of the possibilities of Ex. 37, Beethoven brings the music to an abrupt halt. Three hammer-blows by the whole orchestra arrest our attention.

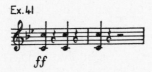

Tentatively, the pattern is repeated a semitone higher. The intellectual in Beethoven has dictated a strange and disturbing shift of tonality; the emotional effect is to translate us into a new world, as magical as any that Peer Gynt may have entered on his journeys. As graceful as an enchantress the second subject appears —or what we are justified in believing to be the second subject.

This theme is in D♭ major, and its key-note of D♭ soon becomes the crucial minor third of B♭ minor—an easy step towards the original key of B♭ major in which Ex. 37 again appears in the somewhat perilous version already shown as Ex. 40. Further exploration of its possibilities brings us to a display of bombast by the full orchestra which is calmed by a last allusion to Ex. 39, now happily wedded to Ex. 42.

Ex. 43

Two resounding chords of B♭ major awake the soloist from his reverie.

The entry of the piano is an entirely logical development of the traditions established by Mozart; a new theme, never even remotely suggested by the orchestra, and in no way attempting to impress us by weight or volume since these were the least striking qualities of the early pianos. What is perhaps un-Mozartian is Beethoven's use of the highest register available to him. The F an octave higher than the top line of the treble stave was a risky note that Mozart hardly ever used—indeed most of the keyboards of the time stopped at the E a semitone below. Its quality must have been thin and it is unlikely that it ever kept in tune for any length of time. The mere fact that Beethoven begins the piano part on this note is evidence of a sort that the instrument had already begun to improve. An elegant little solo leads us by easy stages down to a good fat chord of B♭ major, all in the bass stave. The ensuing phrase in the orchestra, though an unimportant link to Beethoven, interests us greatly nowadays as an early harbinger of his fourth piano concerto. It has the same insistence on repeated notes and a remarkably similar outline.[1]

Ex. 44

The piano brushes this aside and embarks on a busy extension of Ex. 37, indulging in Scarlatti-like leaps and most of the conventional flourishes of early classical pianism.

[1] Beethoven may have 'borrowed' it subconsciously from Mozart's piano concerto in C, K.503, which he almost certainly would have known.

Composers are notorious for their refusal to comply with the examination requirements of academic boards. Hitherto we had been reasonably confident that Ex. 42 was the second subject, but in comparing it to an enchantress I was speaking more truly than I knew. Like most enchantresses she has vanished, leaving only a fragrant memory. 'Here', says Beethoven as the orchestra introduce a new refrain, 'is the true second subject.'

Ex. 45

The pianist tries this out and finds it to his liking, but again the decoration of it is very Mozartian. An abrupt and stunningly beautiful twist into D♭ major restores the true image of Beethoven though, and it isn't long before the pianist finds himself faced with some very awkward passages, with waspish runs and sharp-edged rhythms in each hand in turn.

Apart from giving a bar-by-bar commentary (which would be boring and unnecessary) there is little more that I need to say about this movement. There is an interesting reappearance of the pianist's opening phrases, now in the dominant key of F major. Another point worthy of mention is that Ex. 42, the 'enchantress' theme, does turn up again, although the pianist treats her in a more matter-of-fact way than did the orchestra. Choppy chords in orchestra and piano alike suggest resemblances to the finale of the 'Moonlight' sonata, but the importance of such oblique relationships is an illusion. What is perhaps a comfort to the analytically minded is Beethoven's ultimate affirmation that Ex. 45 is in fact the genuine, true, and guaranteed unmistakably authentic second subject. It happens like this.

At one moment we reach what is clearly the recapitulation. The orchestra pick up the identical phrases which had begun the work; Ex. 39 is assigned to the piano, but apart from a few decorative arpeggios things remain much as they were. But at approximately the place where we might have expected some reference to the hammer-blows of Ex. 41, Beethoven leads directly to Ex. 45 and the enchantress, for all her beguiling appearance, is never heard of again.

The second movement begins rather as though Beethoven had just returned from a performance of *The Magic Flute*, and was recalling the solemn music of Sarastro. It is in no way a quotation, but the almost religious mood is suggested in terms that are remarkably near to the language of Mozart. The piano writing is much more complex in decoration than any movement in a Mozart piano concerto however, and bars which have no less than 36 demisemiquaver triplets in them look bewildering to the eye to say the least. The movement is an extension of Mozart's language rather than a denial of it, and passages like this clearly reveal their ancestry.

Ex.46 Adagio

But whereas some of his contemporaries were producing empty imitations of Mozart's style, Beethoven had the individuality to bend it to his own will, and there are many passages that are stamped unmistakably with the hallmark of his genius. Of these the most conspicuous is a sort of anti-cadenza near the end of the movement. The indication *con grand' espressione* shows us Beethoven's intentions, and while the orchestra recall the very first phrases of this adagio, the piano interleaves with them profoundly expressive figures of this pattern, in the unadorned simplicity of single notes.

Ex. 47

The finale of the concerto begins with the piano in a very skittish mood, presenting a tune which the orchestra takes to most enthusiastically:

Ex. 48

Having even outdone the soloist in a display of exuberant enjoyment, the orchestra seems to pause and take thought; with an almost ecclesiastical gesture they pronounce this solemn phrase:

Ex. 49

The piano part, unimpressed by the change of mood, has a brief clatter of broken octaves that sound to my ear more like an irrepressible fit of the giggles. The orchestra, not amused by this rebuff, re-affirm Ex. 49, whereupon the piano goes dancing off on its own until almost shamefacedly the strings consent to join in with a sort of 'pom-ching' accompaniment.

Beethoven now introduces a new tune:

Ex.50

Like a mocking child giving an exaggerated imitation of a friend's walk, the orchestra give out a derisive version of this phrase. It is Beethoven's way of making the 'wrong note' joke that is the stock-in-trade of so much musical satire. The spirit of mockery is the same whether we find it here in this movement or in Poulenc's *Mouvements Perpétuels*. What we need to do is to clean our harmonic palate enough to be able to appreciate the spiciness of Beethoven's harmony; to regard it as ordinary in comparison to the more exotic fare of more recent years is less than just. Anyway, this slightly grotesque dialogue continues until the pianist in a burst of high spirits starts to play a game that involves hopping a step further each beat.

Ex.51

The split note at the top is part of the fun, giving an impression of fumble-fingered inaccuracy that is denied by the agility of the subsequent passages. These show some inspired extra frills that ultimately reduce the orchestra to an awestruck silence. Not until the pianist has condescended to repeat Ex. 48 can they be persuaded to join in again. At this point things take a more serious turn, and for a moment or two the orchestra builds a climax on some well-used clichés of classical rhetoric. This is too much for the piano altogether; in protest against this unwanted eruption of academic jargon it resorts to a sort of eighteenth-century boogie:

Ex. 52

Once again we have a contrast between the irreverence of the piano part and the rather sober comments of the woodwind, who seem not to approve of these new-fangled high jinks at all. Between each new outburst from the piano we find a self-righteously proper phrase from oboes and bassoons; I need hardly say that it has no effect on the irrepressible high spirits of the piano. Impudence beats dignity every time.

As the movement progresses much the same material appears again, although there are some enchanting new twists in places. One particularly delightful moment comes when the orchestra have been silent for a few bars. The pianist seems suddenly to notice their absence and in a couple of rising phrases seems to say 'Don't you want to play?' The impassive silence that greets each query is a perfect example of the subtlety of musical humour. Finding no response, the pianist proceeds to upset the balance of the tune by transferring the accent into a different place, changing '*Hum*pty *Dum*pty *sat* on a *wall*' to 'Hump-*tee* Dump-*tee* sat ON a wall'. The orchestra express some interest in this, whereupon the pianist prevails upon them to join in once again.

Most beguiling of all is the last page, where the piano seems to cheep like a sparrow in a perky comment on the orchestral tune. The music fades away into virtual silence, broken only by tiptoe chords from the keyboard. Two quiet chords from the orchestra show them entering into the spirit of this game of grandmother's footsteps. Then with a sudden shout of triumph, 'CAUGHT you!', they explode into an *ff* cadence that only serves to underline the humorous content of the whole movement. No music can do so much to destroy the popular misconception that a composer uses music as a means of reflecting his mood of the moment; it is only in Hollywood that a composer needs to feel sad to write sad music and exalted to write exalted music. Here is the music of a sick

man, written under great stress; yet its character is one of capti-
vating gaiety, infecting us all as we listen with its exuberance and
vitality.

CHAPTER V

BEETHOVEN

Violin Concerto[1] in D major, Op. 61 (1806)

1. Allegro ma non troppo. 2. Larghetto. 3. Rondo: Allegro.

Orchestra: 1 flute; 2 oboes; 2 clarinets; 2 bassoons; 2 horns; 2 trumpets; 2 timpani; strings.

THIS WORK, surely one of the two greatest violin concertos ever written, took even longer than usual to be accepted by the musical public. Its first performance was singularly unfortunate; the orchestra was sight-reading without a rehearsal—even the soloist didn't really know it, and it was regarded as so long and diffuse that the audience would get bored hearing it all at once. Consequently the first movement was played in part one of the programme, and the Larghetto and the Finale in part two. In the middle of the concert the audience was regaled with a sonata for violin, to be played on one string only with the instrument held upside down. This circus trick was probably regarded as much more remarkable than the concerto—certainly the violinist had practised it more assiduously since it was his own composition. The next day, the critic of the Vienna paper wrote:

> Among other excellent pieces the remarkable violinist Clement also played a violin concerto by Beethoven which, owing to its originalities and wealth of beautiful passages, was received with exceptionally great applause . . . The opinion of connoisseurs . . . admits that it contains beautiful passages but confesses that the context often seems broken and that the endless repetition of unimportant passages produces a tiring effect.

[1] Beethoven also made an adaptation of this work for piano and orchestra in a bid to increase its popularity.

I like that bit about '*also* played', as though the concerto was a
rather light encore. However, despite the 'exceptionally great
applause' Beethoven had the greatest difficulty in even getting the
work published: several printing houses turned it down, and no
full score was actually engraved until 1894, 88 years after it had
been written. As for performances, various violinists attempted
to popularize it, but all were met with indifference until Joachim,
as a twelve-year-old prodigy, performed it with Mendelssohn
conducting.

I suppose one of the reasons it was slow to catch on is that it is
difficult without being showy, and that much of it takes place in a
world of serenity and peace that is at odds with the rather brash
exhibitionism associated with the nineteenth-century concerto.
It is to violin concertos what Beethoven's fourth—the G major
one—is to piano concertos; and just as that began unexpectedly
with the piano playing quietly and alone, so this begins with four
undemonstrative taps on a drum:

The subsequent phrase on the woodwind is the most important
theme in the movement, firmly establishing the tonality of D
major and conveying a feeling of tranquillity that is the most
noteworthy feature of the work. A balancing phrase leads to the
first string entry, a four times repeated D sharp on the violins about
which any amount has been written already—and deservedly so
since it is a remarkable example of Beethoven's individuality. To
understand its full significance one must realize how important a
sense of key was in Beethoven's time. This concerto is in D major,
and to move out of that key into another one is a form of musical
drama every bit as important as any *fortissimo* climax. The note

D sharp is a rank intruder in the scale or key of D major, and
Beethoven as it were flirts with danger when he now gently
insinuates it into the musical texture. The rhythm he uses refers
back to the opening drum-beats, but the note itself is an outrage
to the whole concept of D major. The other strings react in a
fascinating way—it's as though they were trying to cover up for
the indiscretion committed by the first violins. 'It's D major we're
supposed to be in,' they seem to say, and they reassert the key by
playing the dominant seventh quite strongly. Beethoven again
persists in his gentle tugging at the sleeve of D sharp, and again the
music brusquely regains its balance in a satisfying cadence back
into D.

Ex.54

The woodwind now restore order by playing some straight-
forward scales of D which first climb up and then dip, only to
climb again. All seems peaceful enough when a sudden *ff* from the
full orchestra catches us by surprise. Beethoven cuts right across
the pleasant and pastoral country of D major, and with a violent
change of mood bursts into the fairly remote key of B flat. As a
result of this excursion the surface of the music remains somewhat
ruffled and it's a moment or two before the violins again calm
things down and lead us into the second subject proper. This too
is wedded to the drum-tap motif, which is destined to be of
enormous importance throughout the movement.

Ex.55

Beethoven develops this lovely tune at some length, putting it into the minor and giving it an increasingly complex accompaniment. It is towards the end of this section that one mystery is solved. The baffling D sharp of Ex. 54, which had caused such bewilderment so early in the concerto, is now integrated perfectly into the texture.

As if in triumphant vindication of himself—'You see, I knew it would fit'—Beethoven has a splendid full close in the key of D major, and then several times repeats a new theme of considerable importance.

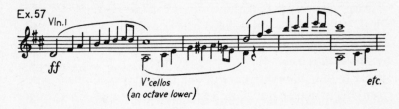

The music dies down and the solo violin is heard for the first time. After so lengthy a preamble it is only right that the soloist should have a share of the limelight straight away, and Beethoven allows the violin to soar high into its most ethereal register before settling down to the matters of the moment with a gently decorated version of the original first subject (Ex. 53). The four drum-beats are usually to be found in the background somewhere, while the orchestra recall the first sixteen bars of the movement in virtually an exact repetition, though now the music is enhanced by decorations from the soloist.

Really to understand how a work of this scale is constructed, one needs to make a bar-by-bar comparison between the orchestral exposition and this secondary exposition involving the soloist.

The first significant change comes with the rising scale-passage that originally appeared on clarinets and bassoons (soon after Ex. 54). Initially this stayed firmly in D major. Once it is given to the soloist we find it being twisted away into new directions, and there is quite a display of agility before things calm down and the second subject (Ex. 55) is allowed to reappear. Again it is scored for woodwind, and it is notable that in a violin concerto, orchestral themes are frequently given to flute, oboe or clarinet in preference to the strings, simply because they offer a better contrast to the tone of the soloist. On this occasion the violin obligingly takes over the melody in its highest register, finishes it off, and then embarks on a long and serious passage in triplets, made up for the most part from broken octaves and somewhat angular arpeggios. Meanwhile violins and violas in unison have a quiet think about the possibilities of putting Ex. 55 into the minor. This leads us towards the fairly remote key of C major—remote in that it cancels out C sharp, one of the most powerful influences on the key of D which is the tonal centre of the concerto. Now all of this had appeared in a comparable form in the orchestral exposition. There too the violins had a minor version of Ex. 55 that was markedly similar to this, in outline at least.[1] But the triplet accompaniment, from which later the embellishments of the soloist are due to spring, was very much smoother and more orthodox as a counterpoint. Horns, trumpets and timpani constantly reiterated the drum-tap rhythm of the first bar, and despite the quiet playing that Beethoven demands, we received an impression of firmness and authority. Now all seems changed; in some extraordinary way the music gives an impression of far greater mystery, and the omission of the drum-tap rhythm (which Beethoven doubtless feels we should now be capable of imagining for ourselves) makes the whole phrase seem much less substantial.

A meltingly beautiful reference to Ex. 56 leads us to something of a climax, but surprisingly it peters out into a quiet recollection

---

[1] The difference being, of course, that one is in the 'tonic' minor of D, the other in the 'dominant' of A.

of Ex. 57 which, since its original function had been to conclude the exposition, must now be made to serve a different purpose. Sure enough, Beethoven uses it to start out on a new journey, the 'cellos being mainly responsible for moving us on into new fields. The writing for the soloist is fairly active though relatively unimportant; the firm line of Beethoven's thought is to be found in the orchestra, and the use of themes that by now should be thoroughly familiar makes the whole passage perfectly clear. But soon we are going to be initiated into a secret and mysterious world, and here once again I must stress the significance of modulation in classical music. While I freely admit that it isn't necessary to know the technical terms for these procedures, we must experience their effect. For instance, we have now reached a point where, by all the laws of musical convention, Beethoven would seem to be heading for a nice safe cadence in A. To simplify reading, I will bring the violin part down an octave and close up some of the gaps.

Ex. 58 Vln. solo

This sit-down on A, while certainly gratifying expectation, is entirely predictable. It is at just such moments that a composer of Beethoven's calibre will prefer to avoid the obvious path home. To move into the unknown, he likes to use something that is familiar; the four repeated notes that began the whole work are the key that opens the door into a new world. Beneath the trill in bar 3 of Ex. 58, the violins play an E four times. They are answered by a low and ghostly F natural from the 'cellos and basses. Hypnotized by this spellbinding note, the violins move upward to F themselves, where in hushed tones they are joined by the other strings. It is like a patch of cloud, ominous and grey until the sunlight of A major is reached again. All through these mysterious happenings, the violin has been trilling like a lark far above the disturbing harmonic

changes in the orchestral part. A few gentle scales against a background of sustained chords from the woodwind lead us to another
violent interruption. In a way it is a pity that we should know a
work like this too well, as inevitably some of the surprise we should
feel at such moments is lost. When Beethoven rocks the whole
fabric of the music with a convulsion of this nature we need at least
to be aware of the shock it must once have caused, even if its impact
on our own ears is somewhat dulled by familiarity.

Mind you, it is an interruption that Beethoven himself has
prepared us for; it has already appeared in the exposition, and
to a superficial glance the ensuing pages would seem to be little
more than a re-hash of part of the opening chapter. There are
variants in the orchestration, and passages that had once been soft
are now loud. However, we need to beware of assuming that the
tunes themselves are the only things that matter in music of this
period. Again it is a question of key; Beethoven ultimately intends
to return to the soaring opening phrase with which the violin
had made its first entry. While on the face of it the orchestra seems
to be going over well-tried ground, there is one profound difference. The music is turned away from the expected home
territory of D major and ends up in C instead. We know therefore
that all is not what it seems and that this, far from being a true
recapitulation, is rather going to lead us still further afield. So it
turns out. A brief cadenza, closely resembling the one which the
violin had originally begun with, leads us to a long development
of bars 2-5 of Ex. 53. The thematic interest lies for the most part
in the bassoons. The strings constantly remind us of the four
drum-taps, while the soloist indulges in very much the same sort
of decorative figures that one might find in a Mozart keyboard
concerto. The music seems to grow in intensity, and then, at the
very moment when we feel that it is going to emerge from the
shadows, it grows quieter still, settling down into G minor. The
horns play four repeated D's beneath a trill from the solo violin and
there begins one of the most beautiful pages that Beethoven ever
wrote. This extraordinarily romantic section is as expansive as a
Chopin nocturne and yet as simple as something by Mozart. All

the time, like a restraining hand that keeps this idyll relevant to the movement as a whole, the horns quietly reiterate the four repeated notes with which the work began. Not only is this the emotional core of the movement; it also fulfils a valuable architectural function, for in its course Beethoven finds his way back to the tonal centre of the piece. Slowly the soloist climbs back towards daylight and the final confirmation of the long awaited D major. This is a moment of triumph, and Beethoven hammers home its importance by asking the whole orchestra to play those first repeated drum-notes. The serene mood of the opening is quite forgotten in this impassioned reprise.

In many points of detail the ensuing pages are different from the original statement of the material; but the big surprises are over. Still to come, though, is one of the most original moments of all, the re-entry of the orchestra after the cadenza is finished. Beethoven never bothered to write out a cadenza, as Mendelssohn and Tschaikovsky did in their violin concertos. There are at least thirty in existence now from which violinists can choose one that suits them best; the most played is one by Joachim, but the cadenza by Leopold Auer runs it close in musical ingenuity. The one significant lead that Beethoven gave was that the cadenza should end quietly, for after the concluding trill he gives the violinist another chance to browse over the lyrical second subject (Ex. 55). The accompaniment is a mere sketch of plucked chords into which the woodwind instruments gradually interpolate a more sustained line. A solo bassoon reminds us of Ex. 57 once more, and then with a brief flourish the movement is over.

The slow movement is a remarkably strictly organized piece of music that still manages to sound like an improvisation. Beethoven accomplishes this paradox by choosing a theme that moves by such gradual steps that we are scarcely aware of any real forward impulse at all. Above it he places a number of profoundly expressive decorations which sound as though they were spontaneous inventions on the part of the soloist. Tovey describes it as one of

Beethoven's cases of 'sublime inaction'. The theme is sixteen bars in length, and full of those pregnant silences which always show Beethoven in his most soul-searching mood.[1]

Ex.59

Larghetto

pp

As one might have expected, these silences are destined to be filled by comments from the soloist. Meantime the theme is repeated with virtually no alteration other than its scoring. The plan of the movement is this:

   I. Theme on strings only.

  II. Theme on horns, clarinet and strings while the soloist adds decorative figures high above (Var. I).

 III. Theme on bassoon, violas and 'cellos with still more complex decorations from the soloist (Var. II).

 IV. Theme on orchestra, quite strongly, but without soloist (Var. III).

So far the form has been so circumscribed as to seem positively restricting, were it not for the beauty of the theme and the marvellous freedom of the solo part that lies above it. Beethoven now has an inspired moment of unorthodoxy. He has given us enough to make us assume that we are listening to a strict set of variations, but now a simple cadenza leads us to a completely new theme. To call this Variation IV would be too far-fetched altogether, although one can force it into the framework of the first four notes by Procrustean methods.

---

[1] Cf. the slow movement of the piano sonata in E♭, Op. 7.

E

Ex. 60

This type of analysis can prove practically anything. However, attractive though it is to those of us who are anxious to twist the evidence to suit our purpose, I refuse to believe that Beethoven intended any such relationship. This theme is an interlude whose function is to create a mood of even greater stillness than before, as well as to focus our attention on the soloist for the first time in the movement. Up to this point the music he has had to play has been purely decorative; now he has a theme, and to catch our interest it is a new theme. Once the point has been made we return to the original idea, and Variation IV appears. Plucked strings remind us of the outline of the tune while the solo violin plays a lagging version above, so drugged with beauty that it can scarcely bring itself to move to the next note. Another short interlude follows, at the end of which the soloist recalls Ex. 60, caressing it with loving embellishments before returning once again to the preceding interlude. We must therefore add these further sections to the plan above:

V. Brief accompanied cadenza, leading to—
VI. New tune on solo violin.
VII. Var. IV on plucked strings with soloist following like a shadow.
VIII. Interlude.
IX. Elaboration of VI.
X. Return to VIII.

This last section seems about to dissolve into nothingness when muted horns followed by violins remind us once more of the first two phrases of the movement. We are on the edge of Paradise when with a cruel blow Beethoven snatches us back. *Fortissimo* chords shatter the mood irrevocably, and the violin is goaded into a brief cadenza that confirms that it too must come down to earth. That Beethoven should leave this vital link to the inspiration of the performer seems rash to the point of lunacy, but I suppose he realized what he was doing. At any rate the die is cast, and the violin leads the way into the finale.

Only the 'cellos seem prepared to follow his lead, and the rudimentary accompaniment they provide to the theme is reminiscent of the spontaneous music-making of country-folk in a pub. Delicate and remote though the sounds still are, they contain subtle suggestions of rhythms slapped out by bare hands against thighs clad in well-worn *Lederhosen*. There's a pint of good German beer on the table, and I can't help feeling that Beethoven whistled this tune in such surroundings when it first came to him, rather than imagining the golden tones of a Stradivarius violin in a concert-hall.

Ex. 61

Tentatively the orchestral violins decide that perhaps they would like to play as well, whereupon the whole orchestra comes thumping in with the theme, extending it with rustic divisions that would have delighted Bottom and his artisan friends. In due course the music quietens down and a sense of expectancy is created by a repeated pattern of tonic and dominant:

Ex. 62

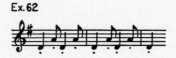

The violinist takes this phrase and throws it high into the air, while underneath a fanfare on the horns suggests a passing group of the gentry bound for an afternoon's sport. As always, I would underline the danger of reading pictures of this type into the music, but Beethoven was not entirely hostile to the idea of pictorial suggestion in his compositions, as the Pastoral symphony and the 'Les Adieux' sonata show. It would be as foolish to deny the obviously outdoor implications of this movement as it would be to try and devise a scenario that would explain them in terms of a plot. The sound of horns may project an image of horse, rider and hound into our minds, but flashing semiquavers from the violin soon bring us back to the world of music, and to a realization that this is no more than an episode in a rondo. For some time the violinist is kept busy with a passage of considerable difficulty, until first the violas and then the violins and 'cellos in turn remind him with increasing firmness that the real matter under discussion is Ex. 61. Sure enough, the soloist takes up the theme once more and for a little while things are just as they were at the beginning.

An ingenious series of modulations brings us to the next episode, a slightly forlorn tune in G minor which one feels should really be attached to a limerick of sorts—

A certain young lady of Bonn
Went to bed with her riding-boots on . . .

Ex. 63

etc.

Such frivolity may seem appallingly irreverent to the ardent Beethoven-lover, but the fact remains that too often we enclose a work of this quality in a sacred casket, making it seem less human than it is. It is Beethoven who decides the content of a movement, not us, and I am convinced that if he had intended a genuine pathos at this point he would not have elected to accompany Ex. 63 with the type of vamped waltz figure that any pub pianist could improvise on the spur of the moment. The minute that he wishes to turn the music in a more serious direction by making it genuinely lyrical, we find sustained chords in the accompaniment and sophisticated ornamentation in the solo part.

Ex. 64

After the first bassoon and the solo violin have danced their way through this section, the strings remind the soloist somewhat peremptorily of the rhythm of Ex. 61. In an amusing weight-lifting contest, soloist and orchestra drag the theme upwards until it regains its proper pitch; once again, Beethoven starts the rondo in its original guise. All goes as one might expect with a substantial recapitulation of most of the earlier material including the hunting horns episode, which is taken over by the entire orchestra to build up a sufficiently impressive entry to the cadenza. This ends with the usual trill, and we are entirely justified in expecting a conventional rounding-off of the movement soon afterwards. (It is worth joining bar 280 to bar 314 to see the sort of thing I mean.) Instead, Beethoven gives us another surprise; 'cellos and basses come in confidently enough with a reference to Ex. 61. Receiving no recognition from the soloist they gradually lose all confidence, getting on to a very false track.

Ex. 65

The violins properly express a certain incredulity about this, but the soloist obligingly meets them half-way by changing the trill from E natural to E flat. All is explained, and the music proceeds quite happily in A flat major, the most remote key from D that it is possible to find. Psychologically this is a master-stroke, for it means that the final return to D will be that much more effective, since the journey back must now be made from the furthest possible point.[1]

An enchanting duet between oboe and violin re-establishes the tonality of D. The mood grows more boisterous and all seems set for a rowdy ending. But Beethoven has one more surprise for us. A sudden diminuendo takes away any suggestion of the uncouth or vulgar. In a moment of supremely imaginative composition we see a glimpse of something of exquisite delicacy, not unlike that fairy world that Mendelssohn was to make so much his own. A last tiptoe version of the theme is given to the soloist, completely without accompaniment, and then two whacking great chords effectively decapitate the movement. It is as though Beethoven had simply said, 'That's enough'; in all his compositions there is no more beautifully calculated an ending than this, the last perfect touch in a work which is as near to perfection as can be.

---

[1] See *Talking about Symphonies*, p. 19.

CHAPTER VI

BEETHOVEN

Piano Concerto No. 5 in E♭ major, Op. 73
(1809–10) (The 'Emperor')

1. Allegro. 2. Adagio un poco mosso. 3. Rondo: Allegro.

Orchestra: 2 flutes; 2 oboes; 2 clarinets; 2 bassoons; 2 horns; 2 trumpets; timpani; strings.

THE VERY different relationship that exists between piano and orchestra in this concerto as opposed to its four predecessors has already been discussed in Chapter I. Right from the start Beethoven establishes the fact that the piano is now on a new footing; it is as though the instrument had finally come of age. Nowhere in the third or fourth concertos do we find passages of a comparable virtuosity—there may be sections that are as difficult to play, but that is not the point; their function is different. What had previously been purely decorative has now assumed the mantle of authority. As for the orchestra, their first few chords reduce them to the level of lackeys opening doors, harmonic doors through which the pianist lets loose a flood of sound. Cascades of notes gush forth from three massive orchestral chords in turn. For a listener of Beethoven's time, brought up on a more orthodox diet, the shock must have been considerable. Revolutionary though this was, Beethoven was not prepared to sacrifice the orchestral exposition as some of the later composers of concertos did. At the end of the third flourish from the pianist, the orchestra take over and there begins an unusually rich and comprehensive *tutti* in which the main themes are all paraded for our inspection. First and most memorable is the characteristic tune which at once establishes a feeling of nobility and heroism.

Ex. 66

Beethoven underlines the importance of this theme by the emphatic accents in the last two bars, and at once repeats it with different orchestration employing brass, woodwind and timpani to make the point doubly clear. The sequel to this phrase will prove to be significant, although at first glance it would seem to be little more than a classical convention of broken chords.

Ex. 67

The lack of padding in this exposition is remarkable considering its length, and each idea must be stored away for future reference as it appears, even passages such as this next one which seems to be a bridge to something else rather than a phrase of any intrinsic importance.

Ex. 68

The second subject, towards which Ex. 68 is a bridge, proves to be a strange little affair, a ghostly march which circles round and round the same group of notes.

Ex. 69

The horns smooth this out into a sustained melody with a gently rippling accompaniment from the strings, when suddenly the music becomes strangely sinister. Nervous fragments of Ex. 66 appear in violins and 'cellos in turn; but with the re-establishment of E flat major all becomes clear again, and Beethoven gives us a substantial development of the first bar of Ex. 66 in particular.

Two more themes are important, one descending and the other rising. Both are based on scale patterns, and once again it is unlikely that if we were hearing the work for the first time we would attach any great significance to either.

We can sense that the exposition is nearing the end as it climbs down towards a final cadence in E flat major; but Beethoven averts the solo entry a little longer yet. One more theme has still to be heard, even though the 'cellos are so impatient to get on that they keep reminding us of the opening figure from Ex. 66. It is a smooth and lyrical phrase in Beethoven's blandest style.

The abrupt final rhythm cuts the melody short and is in turn taken up by woodwind and horns as the soloist enters unassumingly with a long quiet chromatic scale. A sustained trill on a high E flat leads to a singularly calm statement of Ex. 66, now stripped of heroic pretensions and imbued with the classic serenity a composer of Beethoven's maturity knows so well how to impart. Not for long, however; the mood changes, and a series of energetic thrusts explodes into a spattering of chords and octaves that tumble down the keyboard. The music dissolves into a mist of scales backed by quiet harmonies from the strings, until a sharp call to action brings in the full orchestra with Ex. 67.

We shall now see how skilfully Beethoven has planted the basic material of this movement in the opening pages of the exposition. It is always interesting in a concerto to compare the orchestral *tutti* with what I have called the secondary exposition, and never more so than in this magnificently planned work. The two columns in the following table make a comparison between primary and secondary expositions a simple matter, and it will be seen that the 'order of events' is identical in both. Any sense of dull repetition is avoided by the insertion of cushions of new material from the soloist between each of the numbered themes; these introduce that element of fantasy (already mentioned on page 6 of the opening chapter) which is so essential a part of concerto writing.

ORCHESTRAL EXPOSITION (or 'tutti')	SECONDARY EXPOSITION (with soloist)
Ex. 66. 'First subject'. Loud and energetic; played twice.	Ex. 66. Calm and serene; played once and followed by new material from soloist.
Ex. 67. Full orchestra, but with the interest in 1st violins and brass.	Ex. 67. Full orchestra, but then extended by soloist modulating through various keys and changing mood.
Ex. 68. 'Bridge passage'.	Ex. 68. Now in G♭ major and accompanied by decorative figures from soloist. The original ending (not shown in the example) is converted into a short fierce cadenza taking us to B minor.
Ex. 69. 'Second subject'. First version mainly in strings followed by smooth version in horns.	Ex. 69. In piano part followed by a variation in B (actually C♭)[1] major, leading to a very violent version for full orchestra.

[1] See p. 70 Ex. 74.

Bars 57–60 Not shown as a = Bars 174–183 Extended into a music example, but referred to as 'sinister' on p. 63, para. 1.

series of quiet arpeggio figures over sustained chords; sudden change of mood leads to

Bars 62–74 Not shown, but mentioned as development of 1st bar of Ex. 66. = Bars 184–195, a striking passage for piano and orchestra which is also a development of Ex. 66, though far more heroic in character.

Bars 74–78 Not shown, but a = Bars 195–205 Elaborate extension, with the syncopated figure in right-hand part, followed by a complex series of broken chords which finally melt into passage for full orchestra featuring (usually inaudible) syncopations in woodwind.

Ex. 70ᵇ

Ex. 70ᵇ in the piano part; this, extended and then played by the woodwind, brings us to a lengthened version of

Ex. 70ᵇ

Ex. 70ᵇ Quiet descending scales (bars 217–220) lead us to a passage in which the closing rhythm of Ex. 71 is given at half speed—

[Ex. 71 is NOT used here, except for its final rhythm.]

♪ ♩ ♪♩ instead of ♫♩ coming to a powerful and dramatic close in the dominant key of B♭.

It is not until this point that any fundamental change of plan is to be found, and some idea of the relative proportions of the two expositions can be gained by simple statistics. The orchestral *tutti* up to the end of the section of which Ex. 70 is the starting point is 79 bars long, the secondary exposition over the comparable distance consists of 116 bars. The changes have been of two principal kinds, changes of direction involving modulation to more remote keys, and changes of content brought about by introducing the element of fantasy that the soloist brings.

Beethoven now decides to put the clock back, making what may seem a somewhat strange decision about the structure of the movement. For the moment, the soloist is allowed to rest; the orchestra have what is virtually a re-statement of a large section of their original exposition, although naturally it is now in a different key. The passage concerned is similar to the one shown in the preceding table as beginning at bar 62, and it runs on for a further 37 bars until the next solo entry which exactly matches the one with which the first *tutti* had ended. We are on the threshold of the development.

At this point it is worth while to pause for a moment and survey the shape of the movement so far. Basically it is a normal sonata-form movement, although one of great complexity. The exposition alone is over 250 bars in length if we include the primary and secondary versions. Presented in the form of a diagram we now have something like this:

Bars 1–11	Introduction: three 'flourishes'	
Bars 11–111	EXPOSITION I Orchestra only, introducing all main themes	The whole making one sonata-form exposition.
Bars 111–227	EXPOSITION II Piano and orchestra, following same plan, but with extensions and modifications	
Bars 227–268	Reprise of last half of EXPOSITION I	

It is worth noting that Beethoven leads into Exposition II with a long, quiet chromatic scale on the piano which is like the drawing of a curtain. He uses the same device at the start of the development and lastly to introduce the final coda; three of the most significant moments are thus 'unveiled'.

The development begins with quiet and mysterious passages in G major, a less remote key than it would seem since it soon proves to be merely the dominant of C minor—a key which shares the same key-signature of three flats that the 'home' key of E flat major has. Clarinet, flute and oboe in turn now begin a long development of Ex. 66, concentrating on its first two bars and in particular extending the second bar into long and distorted shapes. The atmosphere is almost desolate, the pianist providing a misty background of quiet figuration through which the solo woodwind phrases stalk forlornly. A sudden outburst in F minor brings a tougher mood, more and more instruments joining in as the pianist's arpeggios grow increasingly brilliant. The tension builds to such a degree that it flares into open violence; woodwind and horns, trumpets and timpani fiercely declaim a chord of C♭ (B) major to the rhythm ♪♪|♩ ♪♪♩ ♪♪|♩ which will be seen to be derived from the last notes of Ex. 71. For the first time in the history of the piano concerto, the soloist is able to stand up to this show of force as an equal. Yielding nothing, the piano thunders back, ultimately silencing the opposition as it embarks on a series of dramatic scales in double octaves. While Beethoven appears to have accepted that the new piano for which he was writing could match the weight of orchestral tone in *dialogue*, he still seems to have doubted its capacity to make itself heard *above* any substantial sound. Consequently we find in this next passage a fascinating example of a rigged fight. The piano's octaves are marked *ff*, or very loud.

Ex.72

The comparable passage on strings with which this constantly overlaps is marked *p* or soft, with only the peak-note of the phrase loud; even that is qualified by the instruction *fp*, which can roughly be translated as 'look as if you are playing loud but don't.'

Ex.73

p fp

I am completely convinced that we are justified in changing Beethoven's markings here. It is surely evident from the patterns of the music that this section is conceived as a struggle between equals. I would even go so far as to say that had Beethoven ever been able to hear this passage in his own lifetime he would have allowed the orchestra to play louder; with the resources of a modern concert grand available there can be no doubt that he would have welcomed a stand-up fight between the piano and strings. Only when the pianist's octaves begin a long and beautifully graded diminuendo need the orchestra follow suit. The tumult and the shouting die, and for the first time the soloist is entrusted with Ex. 71. For some twenty bars he muses over it, disregarding the ominous mutterings about the start of Ex. 66 with which the 'cellos and violas occasionally disturb the atmosphere. Nevertheless they are to have their way in the end; in a moment the whole orchestra take up the insistent rhythm and we are snatched from a dream-like trance to the harsh reality of bright daylight. Before we realize what is happening we are thrust willy-nilly into the recapitulation.

Here Beethoven plays a master-stroke. Too often, flourishes such as those with which the movement began seem, on mature consideration of the overall shape of the work, to be an irrelevant appendage. Only by truly integrating them into the whole plan can this potential hazard be overcome, and that is precisely what Beethoven does. In even grander terms than before, the three flourishes reappear, this time thickened by sustained chords on the wind which also serve to bind piano and orchestra more closely together.

It would be laborious to produce another detailed comparison between the secondary exposition and the recapitulation—not only laborious but more difficult, since there are greater differences involved. These differences are not so much in the material as in its relative proportions; for instance, there are now a mere eight bars of orchestral music before the soloist re-enters. When he does so, it is with a totally new and expressive development of Ex. 66. What is interesting is Beethoven's decision to take the responsibility for the cadenza out of the soloist's hands. It was the start of a new order, and from now on composers habitually wrote out their cadenzas as an integral part of the work,[1] or dispensed with them entirely. In this concerto, there is a passage of less than twenty bars before the orchestra rejoin the fray, and of those twenty a mere seven-and-a-half are concerned in any way with the display of virtuosity.

Opinions may differ as to where the coda of this immense first movement begins. To my ear, Beethoven achieves a striking balance by once again repeating the last half of Exposition I as he had in the diagram on p. 66. It is at the end of this that the third chromatic scale already mentioned leads to a quiet and shimmering passage of great beauty, and this, if only for the fact that it is new, I prefer to call the start of the coda proper. The long descent accomplished, the music gathers its strength for the last time before coming to a triumphant conclusion; history had been made, for never again would composers feel the need to 'protect' the soloist in a keyboard concerto.

To write a cold-blooded analysis of the slow movement would seem to be an unforgivable act of vandalism. This sublime music presents no problem, except that of comprehending how the human mind can visualize and then transcribe such beauty. However, since it is the purpose of this book to try to see a little

---

[1] The sole important exception is in the Brahms violin concerto, where the composer relied on his friend Joachim to fill the gap.

way below the surface, let us at least catalogue the main events together with their implications. The key is B major, a choice that Beethoven doubtless made for very good reasons. The note E flat, which was of course the tonal centre of the first movement, now becomes D sharp, the crucial major third of B major, and in order to make the relationship quite clear, Beethoven begins his slow movement with this very note. He has already flirted with this key a number of times in the first movement, usually preferring to write it in the somewhat confusing notation of C♭. This is not just an intellectual quirk on his part, but a practical way of underlining those elements that are common to both keys. Here are three scales, of which the first and last are identical on a keyboard whatever their theoretical differences may be. It will be seen that there are no points of resemblance at all between the scales of B and E♭, whereas there are several between E♭ and C♭.

Ex.74

This may seem to the layman to be little more than juggling with notation, but to a composer such distinctions have a practical and sometimes even a spiritual significance.

The first theme, which appears three times in all, is a melody of the most classical perfection.

Ex.75

Beethoven is so reluctant to finish this that he has some difficulty in bringing it to a close; like a fond lover snatching ever one more embrace in parting, he has four cadences in all before allowing the piano to enter. Over a left-hand part of extraordinary restraint, the right hand sings a melody that is half-way between a theme and a decoration.[1] It is a supreme example of the sort of classical doodling that in the wrong hands can be disastrous. Here, by some inexplicable alchemy, it becomes not a slightly disorientated scale over a conventional and pedantic accompaniment, but one of the most exquisitely beautiful passages ever written. In time it flowers into a melody whose rising sequences might run some risk of banality were it not for the beauty of the setting in which they are placed.

Two sighs of contentment from the orchestra translate us into the colder light of D major where the same misty scales cast their spell. The music grows more emphatic, climbing high on spiralling trills until it descends once more to a decorated version of Ex. 75, now appearing for the first time in the piano part. A few bars of seeming improvisation from the soloist lead us to the third full statement of the theme; this time it is accompanied by a gentle bell-like figure from the keyboard which slowly lulls us into a positively hypnotic trance. The music comes to a point of total rest, a long sustained B on two quiet bassoons. Almost imperceptibly the note shifts to B flat, but if we were not wise after the event, we could well believe it to be an A sharp, a note which might indeed take us to a convincing end, albeit an unimaginative and boring one.

Ex.76

In fact Beethoven exploits precisely the same type of harmonic twist that he had used at the beginning of the movement. By

[1] Shown in Ex. 106, p. 93.

changing E♭ to D♯ he had then opened the door to the 'sharp' key of B major; now, by thinking of A♯ as B♭ he reopens the way back to the 'flat' key of E♭, a tonality which he needs to regain for the finale. Very quietly, as though considering for the first time an idea whose implications are by no means fully realized, the pianist puts forward a speculation about the theme of the last movement. Twice the phrase is heard, illuminating the final bars of the slow movement like the first warmth of the sun before its rim appears above the horizon. We are spellbound, as Beethoven must have known we would be; suddenly, and with characteristic humour, he shouts '*Wake* up!' and whirls us into a dance of extraordinary abandon.

Ex.77

One brief portion of this tune (some seven bars later) is worth mentioning in that it is quoted by Schumann in his *Carnaval*. In his March of the Davidites against the Philistines he had no hesitation in enlisting Beethoven's support; he knew it would have been given willingly.

The orchestra is a little laggardly in joining in, but in due course they are galvanized into action, even extending the tune by a substantial margin. The piano re-enters, throwing off a few exuberant scales before introducing a new and particularly delightful theme—one however that is to remain its own preserve entirely.

Ex.78

Tempting though it must have been to give this to the orchestra, Beethoven prefers to keep it exclusively for the soloist. The course of the movement remains remarkably simple to follow, even if it is extraordinarily difficult to play; the rondo theme (Ex. 77) is seldom far away, but its various entrances are divided one from the other by passages of considerable virtuosity. It reappears in keys as diverse as C major, A flat and (most mysteriously) E. One rhythm

of the greatest importance needs to be quoted:

This crops up in a multitude of places and in a variety of moods. Towards the middle of the movement there is a long sustained trill on the piano, and with a wonderfully calculated piece of craftsmanship Beethoven reintroduces the vision of the theme that had initially been suggested by the piano in the closing bars of the slow movement. In its way, it is as notable an example of integration as was the incorporation of the preliminary flourishes into the middle of the first movement.

It seems to be a characteristic of Beethoven to have a quiet passage just before the final triumph; in this movement there is a wonderful contemplative passage when the piano has a series of descending chords over the softly reiterated beat of a drum. The impression given is one of utter contentment coupled with a pleasant exhaustion; for the moment the busy fingers of the pianist need some respite, but this does not mean that all joy has gone out of the music. Then suddenly, 'That's enough of that,' Beethoven seems to say; 'Let's finish the thing off.' And without more ado, he does.

CHAPTER VII

SCHUMANN

Piano Concerto in A minor, Op. 54 (1841-45)

1. Allegro affettuoso. 2. Intermezzo: andantino grazioso. 3. Allegro vivace.

Orchestra: 2 flutes; 2 oboes; 2 clarinets; 2 bassoons; 2 horns; 2 trumpets; timpani; strings.

IT WAS in 1829 that Schumann, then only nineteen years old, first turned his energies towards writing a piano concerto. An abortive attempt in F major was followed by another failure started in the next year. Both works were left unfinished, as was a third concerto which he began in 1833. Thus discouraged, it is scarcely surprising that he should have decided to postpone any further attempt until his technical command had increased, and it wasn't until 1841 that he tried again. This time he simplified his task by writing a one-movement Fantasy for piano and orchestra, something which he may well have felt was less of a challenge to his skill than a full-scale concerto. The truly Romantic composer is seldom at his best in the larger musical forms, and the title of Fantasy gave him a certain freedom which he must have found comforting.

At the time Schumann was writing with extraordinary facility; the desperate battle for Clara had been won and the couple had been married at last after years of opposition and discouragement. He had loved her since she was fifteen; now his dream was realized, and with his twenty-one-year-old bride beside him he was able to fling himself into composition with renewed fervour. In the early months of 1841 he produced his first symphony, an overture, scherzo and finale for orchestra, and then the Fantasy for piano and orchestra which took little more than a week to write. Clara tried it out with the Gewandhaus Orchestra on 13 August of that year but it seems to have made no great impression, and was laid aside.

Three years later Schumann again turned his thoughts towards the combination of piano and orchestra and wrote a Rondo in A major. It was at this point that someone, probably Clara, suggested joining these two movements together by the addition of a third to make a proper concerto. The happy result of this inspired idea was the concerto as we now know it; under the circumstances its unity is remarkable and nobody would ever deduce from hearing the work how curiously it came to be assembled. The first performance of the final version was given on 1 January 1846; strangely enough it still seems not to have inspired any great enthusiasm. Even ten years later, a critic was to write of Clara's performance of the concerto in London:

> The chief novelty of the evening was Madame Schumann's performance of Dr Schumann's Concerto in A minor, which was received with a warmth well merited by the Lady's playing. Because we cannot fancy that the Concerto will be adopted by any performer in London, we will forbear to speak of the composition as a work.[1]

There are none so deaf as those that will not hear!

Since the first movement was designed as a Fantasy there will be little benefit in searching in it for the normal landmarks of concerto form. In fact it is remarkably concise and well-planned, admirably demonstrating that Form is not something superimposed from outside at the behest of musical pedants but a shape which the material itself has much to do with devising. Fantasy or not, Schumann had learned much from Beethoven, as we shall discover presently.

The first note on the orchestra is like a catapult, launching the soloist into a brief flurry of chords which instantly arrests our

[1] H. F. Chorley in *The Athenaeum*, quoted in Nicolas Slonimsky's *Lexicon of Musical Invective* (Coleman-Ross).

attention. In a matter of seconds the orchestra presents us with the
most important theme of the movement.

This is at once repeated by the soloist before Schumann plunges
us into more disturbed waters. Now one of his most notable
characteristics as a composer is his great flexibility of rhythm, a
flexibility which at times can be positively misleading. Since we
shall find a number of examples of this in the concerto, it will be
worth while to consider the very next phrase from this point of
view. Here is the melody as Schumann wrote it; below it, the
numerals indicate several different ways of 'thinking' the tune with
regard to rhythmic stress.

Certainly it seems a more natural solution to place the stress on
the minim E both times, treating it as the first beat in each case; but
ambiguity could hardly go farther. Gradually a brief but significant
phrase emerges from this deliberately vague background:

In time this is taken up very strongly by the full orchestra while the piano writing becomes more virile with two short octave passages. We then find a long and expressive declamation by the pianist in a rhythm which may well remind us of Beethoven's fourth piano concerto—a work with which this has a certain amount in common. Ex. 79 reappears, now in the more confident guise of C major, until a positively Wagnerian sequence of descending phrases brings us to what might be called Chapter II. (The movement actually falls into nine sections, so we may as well think of them as chapters.) This consists of a long and free develop- ment of Ex. 79 in which the thematic interest is largely in the clarinet. Only the first part of the theme is used, the tail-end being changed to a rising leap of a tenth.

Ex. 82

The piano part meantime gallops along in a characteristic figuration; gradually out of this accompanying pattern a theme grows: to start with one can hardly put one's finger on it, when all of a sudden one is aware that the piano part has become increasingly lyrical, even although its bustling arpeggios have not ceased. Nowhere will you find this theme written out in the exact terms in which it appears as Ex. 83, but this is the sound that the ear picks out even though the eye may not be able to trace it.

Ex. 83

etc.

This rhapsodic interlude ends with a further statement of Ex. 82 from the clarinet, at the end of which an oboe introduces a variant of Ex. 81ᵃ. An interesting example of the way a composer's sub- conscious mind works is to be found at this point. The piano is

shortly to introduce what I am fairly convinced Schumann
believed to be a new theme, but it would seem to be derived from
Ex. 81 despite its apparent differences. The link lies in three notes.

Ex. 84

Thus do fairly large musical oaks from very small acorns grow.
The new theme builds up to an exciting climax on the orchestra in
which yet another variation of Ex. 81ª appears in triumph;
gradually the music climbs down until a gently rocking figure is
all that is left. The mood changes and Schumann embarks on what
amounts to an extraordinarily beautiful Nocturne for clarinet,
piano and strings. Needless to say this is entirely suitable for a
fantasy, if a mite unorthodox in a concerto movement. It is far
from irrelevant, however, since it is a skilful development of
Ex. 79. This then is Chapter III, in which a new light is shed on a
familiar character, and in which, were we to think of it in terms of
Dickensian chapter-headings, 'our hero has an amorous encounter
in the moonlight'.

Now I said earlier that Schumann had learned from Beethoven
in this concerto; we have now reached a moment that demonstrates this. We have seen in the previous chapter how Beethoven
integrated his three opening flourishes into the movement by
introducing them on an even grander scale midway. Schumann
employs the same device. That first brief flurry of chords that had
preceded Ex. 79 at the very start of the work now reappears in a
sudden and violent entry that shocks us out of the trance that
Chapter III has induced. For a few moments there is a hot argument
between orchestra and piano, each vying with the other until a
cascade of octaves from the soloist quells the orchestral opposition.
Chapter IV then is by no means uneventful, even though it is the
shortest episode in the movement. The excitement is maintained
throughout the next section—Chapter V, to continue the analogy
—in which our hero would seem to go for a wild ride in the woods.

One would hesitate to use such words about the music of a truly classical composer, but Schumann was very much the Romantic, his imagination being fired as much by literature and painting as by music. So many of his works bear titles that indicate some extra-musical stimulus that we have less cause in his case to be wary of dragging in non-musical images. If we wish to be coldly analytical we simply acknowledge that here is a new variation on Ex. 79.

Ex. 85

Passionato; piu animato

Gradually the excitement dies and we find ourselves back at the beginning once more, although this time there is no preliminary flourish, Ex. 79 simply emerging quite satisfyingly from a long-drawn-out descent. For some time the music now pursues exactly the same course as before so that, apart from transposition, Chapters VI and VII are identical with Chapters I and II. But at the very moment when we feel that perhaps the composer has settled into too easy a rut of repetition, we suddenly find ourselves being swept up into a glorious climax that leads us into something quite new. We have reached Chapter VIII, the cadenza, which is, surprisingly enough from this most romantic of composers, a classic model of perfection.

It starts with a seemingly extempore passage in which Schumann suggests most skilfully that the pianist may well be improvising after all. The phrase that he would seem to have invented spontaneously is not as irrelevant as it would seem, however, as a comparison with Ex. 84 will show.

Ex. 86

(ex.84 transposed)   Cadenza

* By a curious coincidence this phrase appears note-for-note complete with the same harmonization in Mozart's fugue in C major, K.394.

The soloist seems to meditate on this for some time before a spectacular passage of flying chords brings us to a series of trills, beneath which Ex. 79 reappears as an expressive solo for left hand. Some last impetuous runs lead in to Chapter IX, with which the story ends—or did so until the last two movements were tacked on. The orchestra take up the thread with a quickened version of Ex. 79, of which Schumann once again uses only the first three notes, and the piano part gallops home to a highly effective if relatively unspectacular finish.

The second movement, the last of the three to be composed, is an enchanting intermezzo in which piano and orchestra enjoy a closely-knit dialogue. If the first movement can be said to be mainly concerned with three descending notes, C B A, this is largely built on a pattern of four rising notes, a pattern which the piano states with beguiling simplicity from the very first bar.

Ex.87

This most elegant conversation is continued for some twenty-eight bars, with the soloist waxing lyrical at times in elaborately curving phrases of great beauty. For much of the movement, however, the piano part is entirely subsidiary to the orchestra. First the 'cellos and then the upper strings sing their way through a most mellifluous melody, whose stanzas are occasionally interspersed with disarming phrases on the piano.

Ex.88

The serenade continues, with an especially melting effect when the violins take the melody from the 'cellos as it rises beyond their convenient compass. The opening dialogue is resumed and finally disintegrates. It is at this moment that Schumann brilliantly solves the problem of joining up the last two movements to the Fantasy written three years before. Once again his model seems to have been Beethoven's fifth concerto—those wonderful closing bars of the slow movement in which the piano seems to see the theme of the finale in a golden glow before it bursts into life.[1] Now this is a *forward* look, and if Schumann had copied it exactly, his slow movement would have ended with an anticipation of the finale, something on these lines perhaps:

Ex. 89

I would even hazard a guess that something of the sort may have passed through his mind. His real problem, though, wasn't to link the last two movements but to join them to the first. Suddenly the inspiration must have come to him; instead of Beethoven's forward look, his was to be retrospective. And so we have the lovely moment where the orchestra looks back to the main theme of the first movement (Ex. 79), only to put aside such nostalgic memories and burst through into the exultant finale.

This is a movement of great brilliance and gaiety. For the pianist it is enormously difficult, not so much for its technical demands as for its somewhat repetitious sequences in which it is very easy to take a wrong turning. Orchestra and piano frequently have to play so much 'across' the beat that it destroys all confidence to look at the conductor, whose gestures often seem to be entirely

[1] See p. 71.

disassociated from the sounds that we can hear. The themes are clearly differentiated one from the other and not even the most dyed-in-the-wool Philistine could claim that this movement was difficult to listen to. It begins with a trumpet-like fanfare in which the piano speaks to us with tones of brass.

Ex. 90

These athletic leaps across the keyboard are most exhilarating in their effect, and the rhythmic vitality of the music is enormous. Soon the piano embarks on a long *moto perpetuo* whose span grows increasingly wider the further it goes. At last the music spins to a stop, whereupon the orchestra present the second main theme—another splendid example of Schumann's rhythmical ambiguity.

Ex. 91

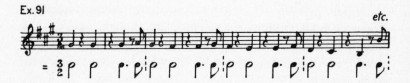

The fact remains that had he used the more logical notation I have indicated beneath, something of the bounce might be lost. As it is, a powerful amount of sniffing on silent first beats goes on in the early stages of rehearsal.

The piano chatters on gaily against fragmentary syncopations from the orchestra until suddenly Ex. 90 bursts back into the fray. Having convinced us of its heroism, it retires into a bookish study and becomes (of all things) the basis of a fugue. This worthy exercise in counterpoint soon loses interest for Schumann, however, and is displaced by a new melody, first heard on the oboe.

Ex.92

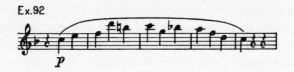

The piano seizes on this happily, sometimes overwhelming it with rushing arpeggios and sometimes babbling away in its upper register.

It is the horns who finally put a stop to this by recalling Ex. 90 once again, the piano part meanwhile grumbling mightily about being taken from the ballroom to the parade-ground. Something like a recapitulation ensues, the music being for the most part transposed up a fourth. It is in the following section that the soloist can most easily go astray, as inevitably his fingers suffer from a feeling of 'I have been here before'. The sequences pound on with the energy of a fast-running tide, the notes rising and falling in wave-like patterns. Finally, by one of those nice, almost mathematical coincidences which music seems to abound in, we find ourselves triumphantly back in A major once more with Ex. 90 reigning supreme. A brief rest for the pianist allows him to gather strength for the coda, which is unashamedly a waltz. In some of the most enchanting music ever dignified by the name of concerto, the notes whirl on, circling and dipping like a ballerina, the orchestra occasionally interjecting fragments of Ex. 90, now wearing its dancing shoes.

Ex.93

Notice that although the piano-leaps are here turned downwards instead of rising, this does nothing to lessen the exuberance of the music. Now and then delicious fragments of waltzes flash past, beguiling the ear, until a last authoritative passage brings the concerto to a stirring close. The whole work has been quite unlike any other concerto and every note is clearly stamped with Schumann's very personal style. If for instance he had never bothered to write the second movement, I am sure no other composer would have conceived anything on the same lines. Yet if we are seeking for comparisons it can truly be said that this concerto is the Romantic equivalent of the last truly Classical concerto, Beethoven's fourth. Needless to say, the whole style of Schumann's composition is far more romantic; the orchestra is less important and the moods are more changeable. It is the absence of force that is common to both. The piano prefers to woo the orchestra, often blending with it in an inconspicuous manner, like a dearly loved queen who mixes with her subjects on the most easy terms. The dominating ferocity that we find in concertos such as those by Liszt or Brahms just doesn't appear in the Schumann. Partly this may be due to the fact that Schumann wrote it for the greatest woman pianist of the age; it must not be forgotten though that it was a tribute not of admiration but of love. That this tribute should come from the most poetic of all composers ensures a work that is unique among concertos—perhaps not an Emperor but a most beloved Princess.

CHAPTER VIII

BRAHMS

Piano Concerto No. 1 in D minor, Op. 15 (1854-58)

1. Maestoso. 2. Adagio. 3. Rondo: Allegro non troppo.

Orchestra: 2 flutes; 2 oboes; 2 clarinets; 2 bassoons; 4 horns; 2 trumpets; timpani; strings.

IT IS hard to believe that a guide-book has been published for intrepid English explorers in which are to be found the names of those restaurants in France considerate enough to serve fish and chips. The sad fact has to be faced that the rich delicacies of continental cuisine are not to everybody's taste; nor is the music of Brahms. To some people his compositions remain turgid, sentimental and overpadded, while the music critic of a leading Sunday newspaper even called the Double Concerto sterile and arid. If this be true, welcome sterility. However, the most imperceptive and biased listener would find it hard to use any of these adjectives about the first piano concerto. It is spare, lean, taut, athletic, certainly not sentimental, and intensely dramatic without ever resorting to the empty gestures of rhetoric. Its initial reception, which was cold and hostile, must have been a bitter blow to Brahms; the general complaint was that the music was dissonant, eccentric and without melody, although in all fairness it must be added that some of the opposition to the work appears to have been dictated by considerations other than musical. Brahms wrote to Clara Schumann describing the first performance at Leipzig:

> My concerto went very well. I had two rehearsals. You have probably already heard that it was a complete fiasco; at the rehearsal it met with total silence, and at the performance (where hardly three people raised their hands to clap) it was actually hissed.[1]

[1] Quoted in *Brahms—his Life and Work* by Karl Geiringer (Allen & Unwin).

Now it is certainly true that the audience would have been expecting something more in line with the fashion of the day, a work in which there would be at least some concessions to surface glitter and virtuosity. There are no such compromises in this concerto, and in effect it is more like a symphony for piano and orchestra than a concerto in the Lisztian manner. Perhaps this was inevitable since the music was originally planned as a symphony. Brahms had a tremendous struggle getting to grips with this piece, and when the first monumental theme came to him he saw it as the start of a purely orchestral work. With much labour he sketched out the three movements, and as composers often do he laid out this first score for two pianos, to save time and effort as much as to be able to try it out. It is what is called a short score, the music being on four staves instead of twenty-four, while instrumentation is suggested by abbreviations such as 'Vn.' for violins or 'W.W.' for woodwind. Conceived as it was at the piano, pianistic figuration kept breaking through; hard as he must have tried, Brahms could not restrict the texture of the music to purely orchestral terms, and what you might call his 'manual imagination'—the sense of what hands can do on a keyboard—kept getting the better of him. The work was re-cast as a piano concerto and ultimately, after much revision, appeared in the form we know today. Its symphonic origin still shows in its almost total denial of the conventionally showy passages in which the later nineteenth-century concertos abound. In concertos such as those by Liszt, Grieg, Mendelssohn or Tschaikovsky, we invariably find the soloist asserting his dominance at an early stage. Not so in the Brahms, where, after an unusually long orchestral introduction, the piano enters with a calm and undemonstrative theme whose spirit is nearer to the spirit of the St Matthew Passion than the glamour of the concert-hall.

We have seen how the Schumann piano concerto was influenced (however indirectly) by Beethoven. The link in this case is much clearer, for the first movement is in the direct line of descent from Beethoven's ninth symphony. Apart from the similarity of key, the emotional resemblances are very strong, and it is an instructive

exercise in musical aesthetics to hear the first movement of
Beethoven's Op. 125 immediately before listening to the Brahms
first movement.

The work begins with an awe-inspiring rumble on drums,
horns, 'cellos and basses. The subject is a magnificent one, torn by
convulsive trills and shouting defiance at a thundery sky.

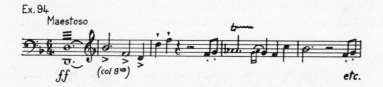

The bass shifts down a semitone to C sharp and the trill theme
becomes the subject of a tug of war between various sections of the
orchestra. The tension increases until at last the music explodes into
two great chords from which there emerges a strange sad theme,
apparently unrelated to anything we have heard so far and as bleak
as Sibelius in his most forbidding mood. The texture is utterly
unlike anything that had ever been written before, so gaunt and
austere does it seem. Skilfully Brahms integrates this new idea with
the first pages by a subtle relationship with Ex. 94; compare these
two figures and you will see what I mean.

Here is the theme that is laid above this bare accompaniment.

The one pale touch of sunshine in this grey world—the F sharp in the fifth bar—is quickly extinguished, as can be seen from even this brief example. The phrase continues to reach upward as though our gaze were scanning the forbidding rock-face of a mountain, the eyes rising towards the mist-enshrouded peak. We come now to a very Brahmsian passage in the dark key of B flat minor. The orchestral colouring is wonderful here and it is hard to understand the insecurity that Brahms felt about his ability to handle a full orchestra when so early a work shows such masterly originality.

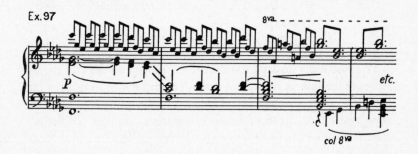

Ex. 97

For some time Brahms seems to brood on this theme, when suddenly our thoughts are violently disturbed by a brutal *fortissimo* and three great hammer-blows from the full orchestra, as though some giant Nordic hero had battered down the door. The opening theme blazes up again with renewed incandescence; it is followed by a terse, abrupt theme in quavers, granite chips from the sculptor's chisel.

Ex. 98

Coupled to this is the one truly optimistic tune of the movement, a call to action that recalls Tennyson's words 'Blow, bugle, blow, set the wild echoes flying'.

Ex. 99

ff

This, harmonized in D major, is combined with both Exx. 95 and 98 in a masterly fusion of ideas. Gradually the excitement dies and the music grows darker once more; quietly and unobtrusively the soloist enters with an extension of Ex. 98.

Ex. 100

etc.

This beautiful and contemplative section continues for some time, but it cannot deny the tremendous forces which it has momentarily tamed; a long-drawn crescendo extending over eight bars leads to a clamorous return of Ex. 94, which storms from piano to orchestra and back again. Here in musical terms is the tempest from King Lear, and its impact is overwhelming. For a few bars the orchestra rages by itself, the next entry of the piano being one of the strangest bits of keyboard writing ever to have come out of the nineteenth century. In the right hand we find Ex. 96, but it is accompanied by a gawky angular figuration in the left hand which is notable for its avoidance of any suggestion of softness in the harmony. It is as bare and uncompromising as even Stravinsky might wish it to be. We are in the throes of the secondary exposition and need feel no surprise at the arrival of Ex. 97, now decorated, as might be expected, with additional notes from the piano. A series of rising trills leads us to a sudden patch of warmth; the comparative oasis of F major has been reached and Brahms is ready to introduce his second subject, a glorious melody which up to now he has kept concealed. It is the soloist's privilege to reveal this treasure:

Ex.101

Although Brahms clothes this in rich harmony he has not conceived it in entirely vertical terms, and the left hand frequently follows the curve of the melody like a shadow. At one point in this long and expansive line there is a possible reference to Ex. 98, now smoothed out almost beyond recognition, and then the soloist embarks on a version of Ex. 99 which climbs ever higher until, like Icarus, it has to fall once more. A brief interlude in D flat major allows us to draw breath before the orchestra in its turn takes over Ex. 101. It is in a somewhat truncated form which soon breaks out into a series of fanfares based on Ex. 99; meantime the soloist chatters away in swift-running thirds. For several pages Brahms occupies himself almost entirely with Ex. 99, moving through various keys before he settles once again into F major. Its softening influence has brought warmth and tenderness in its wake, so that even Ex. 97 now seems to have thawed, losing its grey and forbidding look in a beautiful orchestral cadence.

The new mood is suddenly shattered by an outburst from the piano in double octaves—the only conventional concession to virtuosity in the movement; it begins with a pattern taken from Ex. 99, so that even this is relevant to the issue. A long development of the opening theme follows in which the angular and choppy writing for the piano, while being ungrateful to play, is strikingly effective. Ex. 96 is also extensively discussed by piano and orchestra together, one passage being possibly the first occasion where a composer has written a simple unison tune of this type in a concerto.

Ex.102

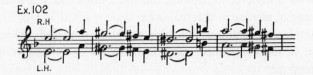

This is a device much favoured by more recent composers, and examples by Rachmaninoff or Bartók come to mind readily; unison passages in Beethoven's fourth concerto are not directly comparable as their function is not so purely melodic as it is here.

Another interesting development is Brahms's new treatment of Ex. 97 which, by a process of compression, becomes very much more energetic in character.

Ex.103

This is so much to the taste of the orchestra that they turn it into a suggestion of a waltz, while the piano part, momentarily released from the brooding and thunderous atmosphere which pervades the rest of the movement, indulges in some delightful and light-fingered passage-work which is a welcome patch of sunshine in an otherwise sombre composition. The passing happiness is not long-lived, however, and a sudden dramatic build-up leads us to some tremendous chords. We have arrived at the greatest moment of the whole movement, the recapitulation. Brahms's avoidance of the obvious here is sheer genius. Everything converges on the home note of D, and not unnaturally we are expecting the theme to reappear as it originally did in Ex. 94, starting on B flat. The complete unexpectedness of the piano entry on E is one of the great shocks of the entire literature of music, to be compared to the effect of entering a room by jumping through a plate-glass window instead of walking in through the door. The music explodes into greater violence than before, such violence that even the gentle phrases of Ex. 100 are transformed by the orchestra into a passage of searing intensity.

A gradual lessening of the tension brings us in due course to a reprise of Ex. 101 and for a moment or two we can relax again and enjoy the sensuous beauty of this most Brahmsian tune. The

composer has by no means finished with us, though, and before
long we are again caught up in the demonic trills and thundering
octaves that we have inevitably come to associate primarily with
this work. The movement ends as it had begun, 'in thunder,
lightning and in rain'.

The slow movement can be reasonably assumed to be in the
nature of an 'In Memoriam' to Schumann, whose attempted
suicide had been a terrible shock to Brahms. The opening bars
have more than a suggestion of choral music about them; indeed,
Brahms even went so far as to write the words 'Benedictus qui
venit in nomine Domini' over the first orchestral phrase.

Ex. 104

The mood is markedly similar to parts of the Requiem that he
was to write some seven years later.

When the piano does come in, the style of writing is again
extraordinarily original, the conventional clichés of pianism being
brilliantly avoided. Both hands play virtually identical parts,
separated from each other by a gap of an octave. The texture that
Brahms uses here, and even more so in a few later passages, may in
itself be intended as a tribute to Schumann, since it resembles parts
of his great C major *Phantasie*, Op. 17, a work which Brahms
would certainly have known intimately. Such links in no way
detract from the quality of the piece, being matters of influence
rather than plagiarism. Where they can become interesting is in
detecting not similarities but differences between composers. This
second movement provides a classic example of this in the next
piano entry.

Ex.105

It seems to me perfectly legitimate to compare this to the slow movement of Beethoven's fifth concerto as well as to the finale of the Schumann *Phantasie*, Op. 17. Here first is the Beethoven, whose absolute simplicity breathes a spirit of classical purity.

Ex.106

Certainly this is romantic music in that it is deeply felt and expresses a profound emotion. Despite this the idiom remains entirely classical, conveying by its very restraint a special quality that makes it quite different from later, more overt expressions of the same mood. Turn now to the Schumann:

Ex.107

The much greater span of the accompanying left-hand part, the cross-rhythm of three against two, as well as the G sharp in the melody, make this more flexible and more openly romantic. It is the 'warmest', the most personal of the three examples, having neither the restraint of the Beethoven nor the angular distortion—and consequently greater sense of anguish—of the Brahms. Yet on the face of it there are close resemblances between them; each begins with a spread octave, each traces a long and expressive descent in the right hand and each has a simple accompaniment on roughly similar lines.

If we want to find Brahms writing in a way that has no parallel we do not have to look far, for a strange episode soon begins in which a curiously shaped melody rides uneasily above gaunt syncopated octaves and a rising chromatic bass.

Ex.108

It reads rather like an orchestral transcription for piano solo, but in fact it remains the exclusive property of the soloist.

There are several climaxes in this movement, including one magnificent passage of chords leading to a series of wave-like arpeggios, which suggest the prow of a ship dipping and plunging into an ocean swell. A strange and highly original cadenza consisting of loops and swirls of notes ultimately unfolds into the closing phrases from the orchestra which bring this unique movement to its final resting-place.

The finale has in its opening bars a certain affinity with the third movement of Beethoven's concerto in C minor (No. 3). The piano kicks off with the principal theme, strutting tenths in the left hand giving the music a marvellous bounce at times.

Ex.109

In a Rondo, the theme is seldom developed in the true sense of the word; it is used as a landmark to come back to after each of a series of journeys, as though one were staying in a hotel surrounded by walks. The hotel is the Rondo theme which one returns to after each outing; sometimes it may look a little different because of the light but you know perfectly well it's the same hotel.

In this movement, the first 'walk' is quite a long one. After several repetitions of Ex. 109, it begins with a gentle rise until gradually it emerges on to a lovely plateau where we find the second principal theme, a wonderfully relaxed singing tune.

Ex.110

For some time the pianist extends this melody, his left hand assisted by pizzicato 'cellos, but otherwise alone. Only when the excitement has increased substantially do more of the orchestra join in. A quiet interlude follows with the strings rocking gently through a very Schumannesque phrase, when suddenly a suspiciously Wagnerian horn-call[1] summons us, and a precipitate descent back to the hotel begins; after a long unwinding Ex. 109 is safely resumed.

Walk number two takes us through some very beautiful and pastoral country, first revealed to us by the orchestra.

[1] Actually derived from the first three notes of Ex. 109.

Ex.111

Brahms shows his usual mastery of counterpoint in his treatment of this essentially lyrical theme, having any number of shadows and reflections of its outline in the supporting parts. After dallying with it for some time in the most affectionate manner, he suddenly decides to make it the basis of a scholastic argument, as though two professors had stopped in an idyllic setting to discuss the nomenclature of a botanical specimen.

Ex.112

In its way this is as unexpected a development as the fugal episode in the finale of the Schumann piano concerto, to which it bears a resemblance of context if not of material. The pianist tries to inject a little light and cheerfulness into the increasingly academic atmosphere by producing a deliciously lyrical version of Ex. 109— not, as one might say, a return to the hotel, but a reminder of its delights. In due course the main theme is regained, but this time Brahms presents it to us in its most stormy guise. Even Ex. 110 is affected by the extreme severity of the music at this point, translating itself into the minor with striking effect. A Bach-like cadenza, having towards its close passages not unlike some of the writing in the slow movement, leads us to a new version of Ex. 112, now seen in a golden sunset such as Brahms was to create in the final pages of a number of his works. For a long time it even seems as though we are coming to a quiet ending. The music grows slower in tempo, while pastoral horns and oboes start a country dance that is full of old-world charm. A long passage of descending trills drifts quietly downwards like the sound of sheep-bells as the flocks come down the mountain-side. Just as the feeling of twilight reaches the point of nostalgia, Brahms decides to whip up the pace and the last revels begin. A final dance of great energy and excitement rounds off this remarkable work. How could the audience at Leipzig have refrained from applause?

CHAPTER IX

BRAHMS

Violin Concerto in D major, Op. 77 (1877?–78)

1. Allegro non troppo. 2. Adagio. 3. Allegro giocoso, ma non troppo vivace.

Orchestra: 2 flutes; 2 oboes; 2 clarinets; 2 bassoons; 4 horns; 2 trumpets; timpani; strings.

THE OPUS NUMBER 77 indicates that this is far from the youthful work the D minor piano concerto had been; in fact Brahms was forty-five when he started the first draft. Revisions with the great violinist Joachim's collaboration were to take nearly a year, the composer apparently being quite willing to bow to Joachim's judgement on anything to do with violin technique. A letter accompanying a first copy of the solo part reads: 'Of course you must correct it, not sparing the quality of the composition; if you don't think it's worth orchestrating, say so.'

Another letter of a later date tells us that Brahms revised the work extensively, whether as a result of Joachim's suggestions or not we do not know. 'The middle movements of the work are failures,' Brahms wrote; 'I have written a feeble adagio instead.'

The two rejected movements were later used in the second piano concerto; as for the 'feeble' adagio, one can never be sure how serious Brahms was in the frequently deprecatory remarks he used to make about his music. I tend to think that the more pleased he was with a work the more it amused him to run it down. Although Joachim's first reactions to the manuscript were dubious, he cannot have failed to be impressed with the immense scale of the piece. His first introduction to the concerto was, as I have implied, through the violin part alone; he can have had little idea of the richness and beauty of the orchestral introduction, nor of the profoundly satisfactory solution of the problems of relating violin and orchestra to each other, without too obviously rigging the contest in the soloist's favour. A violin concerto is a notoriously tricky problem for a composer, and it is notable that although each wrote more than one piano concerto, Beethoven, Brahms, Tschaikovsky and Mendelssohn[1] all suffered from once-bitten-twice-shy feelings about violin concertos. The technical reasons for this are fairly obvious; it is a difficult instrument to write really virtuoso music for unless you are a first-class performer yourself,[2] and the problems of balancing one violin against an orchestral background containing thirty or forty more of them are considerable. Brahms's solution to the first problem was to seek the help of Joachim in all matters relating to the technical requirements of the solo part. As to the question of balance, that was a challenge to his skill as a composer, a challenge he met brilliantly—the usual criticisms that it was *against* the violin, that it was impossible and so on notwithstanding.

The work begins with such an air of peaceful serenity that we might be on the threshold of a slow movement rather than one of the grandest movements ever planned for violin and orchestra. Violas, 'cellos and bassoons are soon joined by horns in this essentially pastoral theme, the first of the three which together make up the first subject material.

Ex. 113

---

[1] I do not include Mendelssohn's concerto in D minor written when 13.

[2] Composers who were violinists themselves, and who consequently had no hesitation in writing more than one violin concerto, include Paganini, Vieuxtemps, Wieniawski, Vivaldi, Mozart and Bach.

The second element, which immediately follows after this, flirts with C major, thinks better of it and then turns the tonality unexpectedly towards D minor.

Ex. 114

The last note of Ex. 114 is also the first note of Ex. 115, for now we meet the third of these three themes. It is of a much tougher fibre with its strong leaping octaves and its typical syncopation.

Ex. 115

Ex. 113 returns in triumph, the impact of the full orchestra seeming to change its character entirely. Brahms chops out four notes from the theme and worries at them like a terrier. Suddenly the music is arrested in full flight by a single note from horn and oboe and we find ourselves translated as if by magic into the world of the second subject; this too consists of three ideas, the first of which contains one ingredient common to all.

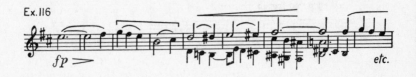

Ex. 116

The five notes contained within the square bracket will readily be seen to be the main component of the next example.

Ex.117

PP

The joining together of these various brief episodes that comprise the second subject group is marvellously subtle in its craftsmanship. We have seen the link between Exx. 116 and 117. Brahms now uses the falling fourth in bar 5 of Ex. 117 as a further bridge, stretching its span by making it into a series of dotted minims (notes to the value of three beats). From this moment of extreme stillness there now emerges another important idea, the third of our trio.

Ex.118

p *etc.*

The eye can perhaps spot even more quickly than the ear the relationship that exists between this theme and its immediate predecessors. It leads us into a dark and mysterious passage of haunting beauty; the atmosphere is hushed and still. The spell is broken abruptly by a fanfare-like theme, imaginatively scored for strings rather than brass in order not to put the soloist at too great a disadvantage.

Ex.119

f *etc.*

This breaks off into a tremendously strong figure in semiquavers beneath whose angry tumult there is a somewhat angular rising phrase, the shape of which has some bearing on the soloist's now imminent entry.

Ex. 120

The eight examples which it has been necessary to quote in order to be able to explore the orchestral introduction show just how concentrated Brahms's thoughts are. Every one of these is destined to find an important place in the scheme of the movement as a whole, and while the *tutti* has seemed exceptionally rich in material there is not an irrelevant or unnecessary note to be found.

With the most electrifying entry ever devised in a violin concerto, the soloist now flings himself into the fray; the mood is heroic, stormy and yet magisterial. It is not easy to realize that these lightning-flashes stem from the gentle curve of Ex. 113.

Ex. 121

The orchestra fling back their defiance with furious snatches of Ex. 119, the first note of the rhythm being amputated to allow the soloist a clear first beat in each bar (see bar 5 of Ex. 121). Battle is truly joined as it had never been before in a violin concerto. A struggle of such intensity cannot be continued indefinitely, however, and it is not long before an extended passage in rippling arpeggios proclaims an uneasy armistice while solo woodwind play sad distortions of Ex. 113. At last, in a translucent shimmer of sound, this first theme returns, climbing its way down through the orchestral strings; peace is restored, and the way is now clear for the soloist to present us with Ex. 113 once again, clad for the first time in those warm and tender harmonies which have been there by implication since its inception.

A brief and ethereal meditation divides Exx. 113 and 114 from each other in the secondary exposition which now begins. The order of events is, as might be expected, comparable to what happened earlier, but there is not a bar that is the same. The original scoring was so felicitous that it is hard to believe that Brahms could improve on it in any way, yet there is if anything an even greater richness of colouring. Meanwhile the soloist provides not only the most sensuously beautiful decoration at times, but a considerable strength as well. Ex. 115 is flailed by the violin, first with strident chords and then with a hailstorm of semiquavers. Gradually this demonic energy is stilled with a gentler figuration that almost caresses Ex. 116, until the rapt hush of Ex. 117 engenders an absolute calm. A distant mutter of drums, and we are gracefully led towards what might be termed the true second subject. Like Mozart and Beethoven before him, Brahms here delights in reserving the most precious treasure for the soloist. Ushered in by the first curving phrases of Ex. 118 a new melody appears; it is Brahms *par excellence*, most especially in the heart-touching tenths (bars 7 and 8) whose emotional impact on the violin far transcends anything that the piano could do.

Ex.122

This radiant theme appears like a newly opened flower, all the more beautiful in its contrast to the sombre phrases which have previously been associated with the first two bars of Ex. 118. Over an accompaniment of the utmost delicacy, the violin has a long and tender extension of the cross-rhythm that ends Ex. 122. The

music turns towards the minor; not to be denied, the sad refrain of
Ex. 118 reappears, supported by gaunt double-stopping from the
soloist—a marvellously calculated effect.

Our memories of the exposition should now tell us that Ex. 119
is not far away, and sure enough it again cuts violently across the
prevailing gloom. Despite its chordal texture it proves to be wholly
suitable for the violin[1], as a knowing ear might have guessed even
from its orchestral presentation. Ex. 120 is now divided between
soloist and orchestra in a passage whose great dramatic force
ultimately explodes into an outburst from the full orchestra. First
and second violins show those of us who hadn't realized it that
Exx. 121 and 113 really were related; trumpets and horns unleash
the most savage version of Ex. 119 that we have yet heard; alternations of Exx. 122 and 118 take us through patches of sunshine and
cloud. In one of the most intensely romantic phrases in the whole
work the violinist takes bar 3 of Ex. 118 and clothes it in black
velvet, a dark elegy even by Brahms's standards. Then, with a touch
of caprice as the orchestra picks up the thread once again, the violin
goes off into a fey little dance, like one of those rather sad fairies in
A Midsummer Night's Dream who are given the less enjoyable
chores at Titania's court. This meltingly beautiful section, which
lasts some twenty bars, is suddenly shaken by a series of stabbing
trills from the soloist. The effect on the orchestra is immediate;
those very pairs of notes which so beguiled us in the preceding
section are seized and torn apart. Was there ever a better demon-
stration of the flexibility of music than this, for the same basic
pattern serves equally well to convey an infinite tenderness and a
savage pride.

A massive chord for brass and wind brings us again to Ex. 115 in the orchestra with the solo part striding ruthlessly across the marching octaves in the bass. If ever the violin has been in the position of a dominant conqueror of the orchestra this is the moment; no one who is the least bit sensitive to music could fail to be thrilled by it. Heroism is not a quality one normally associates with the sound of a violin, but the subsequent octaves (based on Ex. 119) have an unquestionably heroic effect. The bow has become a rapier, the orchestra a swarm of adversaries who must be quelled. This section, culminating as it does with a triumphant return of Ex. 113, is the dramatic core of the movement.

The recapitulation is as orthodox as we might expect it to be in the hands of a composer as classically minded as Brahms. We meet a number of old friends again; but there was never a better example of the significance of transposition than this. For many people, transposition is a technical term that describes some rather vague and mystical aspect of music that can surely be no concern of theirs. They know it has something to do with themes appearing in different keys, but little more. Turn back to Ex. 119 though, and having played it in that key, try it in A minor (Ex. 124). Even on the keyboard it sounds strikingly different, and when we hear the two versions on a violin the additional change of colour that comes about by moving to the three lower strings[1] is remarkable.

Ex. 124

etc.

* In avoiding unnecessary duplication of examples a misleading impression may have been given. The actual *order* of keys is: (1) D minor in orchestra, (2) A minor on violin, (3) D minor on violin. It is these last two that sound so markedly different.

In due course we arrive at a traditionally placed cadenza. It has already been mentioned (p. 69n.) that this concerto is the last truly

[1] i.e. as in Ex. 119.

great work in which the composer was content to leave the
cadenza to the performer; to have done so was the nicest compli-
ment that Brahms could have paid to his friend Joachim. Now it
is only too easy for a cadenza to seem, in the classic phrase of the
American courts, 'irrelevant, incompetent and immaterial'. In
this case it would show an extraordinary insensitivity to the music
to produce a cadenza that was nothing but a virtuoso showpiece.
Throughout the movement the concentration on the material in
hand has been remarkable and there has hardly been a single passage
in the solo part that has not been of genuine thematic interest.
In the circumstances the masterly cadenza that Joachim provided is less of a feat that it might otherwise have been; all he
had to do was to select and rearrange. The one clear lead he had
was that it was essential to finish quietly. The re-entry of the
orchestra is one of the most sublime moments in the whole work;
obviously it must be suitably prepared. It would not surprise me
if Brahms had Beethoven's fourth piano concerto in mind here;
both works have the same quality of a golden sunset at the aftermath of the cadenza, both allow a last concession to virtuosity
in their final bars, blowing up a flurry of notes which dispel the
magic of the quiet passage preceding them. In this concerto it is
Ex. 113 that has its last tender apotheosis at this point; it climbs
higher and higher, attaining a celestial top C sharp before starting
a gradual descent. Themes that have almost dissolved in this all-
pervading warmth gradually reform into more substantial shapes.
The soloist responds to the changing mood, and a brilliant spatter
of double-stopped notes brings the movement to an end. Even this
is not irrelevant, being a more extrovert form of a phrase that has
so far been a gentle counterpoint to Ex. 113.

Brahms originally planned four movements for this concerto,
but the two central movements were dropped, the themes thereof
being transferred to the B flat piano concerto (see p. 98). He was
ever a perfectionist, hating a work to be performed until he was
satisfied that everything was just as he wished. In the event, the

slow movement that he finally wrote is as perfect as any in the
repertoire. Only in the thirtieth bar do the orchestral strings make a
discreet entrance; up to then, the music is scored entirely for wind.
It would be absurd to describe this as a welcome relief from string
tone, but the skill with which Brahms varies his tonal palette by
this discipline is worth mentioning. The oboe takes the limelight
in the presentation of this memorable melody. (The two introductory bars have been omitted.)

Once this tune has run its full course the strings gently remind us
of the two chords with which bassoons and horns had begun the
movement; it is a clue that we should not disregard, for Brahms
now turns back the page, beginning what is in fact an ingenious if
free-sounding variation on the melody just heard. His technique
is a highly sophisticated one, by means of which one bar of the
theme is frequently expanded into two in the variation. It would
be wearisomely pedantic to trace its entire span, but a comparison
of the first few bars should give us sufficient idea of his method.

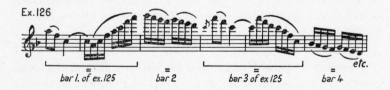

Once we have reached the equivalent of the eleventh bar of
Ex. 125, the music starts to change direction, much use being made

of the supporting chromatic figure shown in the example. It settles somewhat uneasily into F sharp minor, at which point the violin introduces a rhapsodic episode whose sole link with past experience lies in its first three notes,  which are presumably related to the second bar of Ex. 125. But while the violin part may seem to trace its elaborately decorative patterns at will, the orchestra become obsessed with a diminutive version of that same chromatic figure that first disturbed the secure world of F major—bar 11, Ex. 125. Over and over again we hear it, now in the strings, now in the wind, conveying to an increasing degree an anguish of spirit to which the soloist responds in ever widening loops and coils of notes. Some tortuous modulations lead us at last back to F major, a return to normality which allows Ex. 125 to reappear in full once again. Over a serenade-like accompaniment from plucked strings, the solo violin produces a glorious extension of the tune.

Ex. 127

poco a poco crescendo   etc.

It is the last flame before the fire dies; the oboe seems to want to begin Ex. 125 once more, but after a mere five notes the music starts a long-drawn-out descent whose nostalgic cadences suggest that sweet sorrow at parting that Shakespeare expressed so touchingly in *Romeo and Juliet*. Bassoons and horns again remind us of the two opening chords; a last word from the soloist, and the movement is ended.

It must be confessed that finales are seldom the best of movements; so often inspiration seems to flag; so often the determination to be gay and brilliant at all costs leads to a loss of quality in the music. In this work Brahms keeps his astonishingly high standard right to the end. The enormous technical difficulties involved

frightened most fiddle-players away for many years after the
concerto appeared. As always, technique caught up with the
demands in the end—so much so that in the late years of his life
Brahms had the delight of hearing it played by the twelve-year-old
Hubermann.

Having stood in silence for a considerable time at the start of the
two previous movements, the violinist is impatient to begin; for
once, he has the theme 'from the top' as the orchestral players say.
It shows Brahms in that gipsy mood that he so enjoyed.

Ex. 128

The orchestra by common consent agree that this is a splendid
tune, whereupon the soloist expands it a bit further, indulging in
some fearsome exercises in double-stopping as he does so; Brahms's
warning against taking the music too fast must have brought solace
to many a player here. The theme is taken up again by the full
orchestra, who proceed to jazz up the sequence in bars 5-8 in a
somewhat disrespectful manner. Sparkling arpeggios from the
soloist keep the texture as light as a well-made *soufflé*, until the
sudden emergence of a much tougher theme reminds us that this
is a concerto and not a rather high-class café piece.

Ex. 129

It will be seen that the orchestra enthusiastically turn this phrase
upside down as soon as they have cottoned on to it. For some time
the music stays in a pretty stormy mood, but it is an exhilarating

storm, quite free from the menace that Brahms had conveyed so clearly in the opening pages of the D minor piano concerto.

A return to Ex. 128 leads us, after some discussion, to a fascinating new tune, fascinating in its unexpected time-signature of three-in-a-bar.

Ex.130

The strings try to cover up this apparent aberration on the soloist's part with urgently whispered reminders of the 'proper' rhythm in $\frac{2}{4}$; but the soloist persists in this wayward disregard of convention. The oboe betrays his colleagues by finding Ex. 130 very much to his liking and it isn't long before there seems to be a general approbation in the orchestra.

A few flashing scales lead us once more to Ex. 129, and the buffetings of the March gale beat about our heads again. A long and triumphant development of Ex. 128 leads us to a brief cadenza which so demoralizes the orchestra that they can only resort to vague mutterings about the start of the original theme. Meantime capricious little arpeggios and trills from the soloist give the music an elusive will-o'-the-wisp character that is curiously unlike our normal conception of Brahms. For quite a while we have the impression that Ex. 128 is on the brink of returning; it is vaguely reminiscent of amateur theatricals at a village hall. We sit awaiting the entrance of a principal character, our expectations clouded by uncertainty as the audible whisperings in the wings fail to produce any visible result.

A change of tempo, a few train-like chuffs from the orchestra and our theme appears at last, clad in hunting-costume astride an uneasily jogging steed.

The joyful ride home begins. Even Ex. 129 becomes positively frivolous under the influence of these infectious rhythms. Only one surprise remains, and that is on the final page. Taking a last leaf from Beethoven's book (see p. 60) Brahms unwinds the music completely just before the last triumphant chords. Fragments of Ex. 131 drift down like autumn leaves, accompanied by a sad chromatic descent in the woodwind. It would be presumptuous to interpret this in other than purely musical terms; it is simply a vision of a very special type of beauty that reminds us that life is more than beer and skittles.

CHAPTER X

DVOŘÁK

Violoncello Concerto in B minor, Op. 104 (1894–95)

1. Allegro. 2. Adagio, ma non troppo. 3. Finale: Allegro moderato.

Orchestra: 2 flutes; 2 oboes; 2 clarinets; 2 bassoons; 3 horns; 2 trumpets; 3 trombones; 1 tuba; timpani; strings

IT WAS a strange chain of events that took the son of a village butcher and innkeeper from a remote part of Bohemia to the go-ahead world of New York, but Dvořák was one of the happy band of composers who have achieved success in their own lifetime. Recognition came late, but once it did come he was lionized and fêted in many countries. Perhaps the most striking material proof of this fame was the invitation to become the director of the National Conservatory of Music in New York, a post which Dvořák held for three years from 1892 to 1895. While there he wrote seven works of which this concerto was the last; it was written in almost exactly three months, during which time Dvořák worked on it without pause. On his return to his native Bohemia he made substantial alterations to the finale, as a footnote to the manuscript score tells us: 'I finished the Concerto in New York, but when I returned to Bohemia I changed the end completely as it stands here now. 11th June 1895.' The first performance of the concerto was actually given in London on 19 March 1896, Dvořák having had some disagreement with his fellow-countryman Hanuš Wihan, to whom the work is dedicated. Wihan was a renowned 'cellist and made many suggestions to the composer about technical matters; however, when he proposed the insertion of a large-scale cadenza in the last movement, Dvořák had to insist on having his own way. He stated most emphatically in a letter to the German publisher Simrock that he had not authorized anyone to make any changes.

'I told Wihan straight away when he showed me his cadenza that it was impossible to stick bits on like that,' he wrote (3 October 1895). In spite of the quarrel Wihan's name appears on the title-page as dedicatee, though it was not until some three years later that he actually played it in public.

The first problem in writing a 'cello concerto is balance, for it is more or less true to say that the lower the pitch of an instrument the less penetrating its tone is likely to be. One piccolo can make its small shrill voice heard above a vast orchestra; but a solo 'cello is hard put to it to stand out from the orchestral mass. The reason for this is due partly to acoustics, and partly to the fact that our ears are not normally attuned to melodic listening in the lower registers. Dvořák solves the problem magnificently in this work; even in a concert-hall, the 'cello is hardly ever over-balanced. If there are weaknesses in the concerto they occur at moments of self-indulgence in which Dvořák perhaps has one 'dying fall' too many; it needs a cold and unsympathetic ear to spot them, however, and in performance one usually surrenders to the warmth and charm which so pervade this delightful score. When Brahms first came across it he said to his friend Hausmann, 'Why on earth didn't I know that one could write a 'cello concerto like this? If only I'd known, I'd have written one years ago.'[1]

The construction of the first movement is on traditional lines to start with, the main themes being clearly stated by the orchestra. The hues at the beginning are sombre, clarinets in their darker register accompanied by soft chords on the lower strings. The theme makes an immediate impression even though it is still only stated quietly.

---

[1] Recounted by Sir Donald Tovey in *Essays on Musical Analysis*, Vol. III (Oxford University Press).

Ex.132

Violins and violas extend this, stretching the third bar in particular and whipping up a fairly dramatic state of tension in a comparatively short space of time. Within twenty-three bars we find the full orchestra taking part with a grandiose version of Ex. 132; Dvořák makes it abundantly clear that this is a theme of some importance. Suddenly the music breaks off into a shimmering descent with typically bird-like trills on the woodwind. As is so often the case, Dvořák suggests a pastoral outdoor world to us; one feels that he must always have composed with the windows open. 'Cellos and basses recall us to a more severely academic mood with a rising scale-passage that sounds far more important than it actually proves to be; a few wisps of Ex. 132 remind us of the first subject. There is a feeling almost of hesitancy as the strings sigh their way through a long sequence of descending fourths, and those of us who have not heard the work before may perhaps look expectantly towards the soloist. Then from the back of the orchestra there emerges a radiantly beautiful tune; this and the slow movement of Tschaikovsky's fifth symphony must be among the most worth-while moments of a horn-player's life, for it is to a solo horn that Dvořák first entrusts this melody:

Ex.133

The utter simplicity of this melodic line shows one of Dvořák's most beguiling assets. As with Schubert, one feels that composition comes so naturally to him that the song in the bath at eight o'clock goes straight on to the manuscript paper at nine; whereas Beethoven or Brahms might mull over the same idea for days before finally committing it to paper. The danger of so uncritical an approach is that it can on occasion lead to moments of banality. There is an example of this very shortly when the whole orchestra rejoins the fray with a rustic and unpolished tune which I suspect may have caused Brahms to raise an eyebrow when he first perused the score. Even Dvořák may have thought better of it, for it never reappears; it is perhaps more of a boisterous welcome for the soloist than anything else, as though the orchestra were to say, 'Here he comes, let's give him a hand.' The noisy greeting dies down, giving way to a hushed chord of B major whose relative brightness is hardly noticed, so darkly is it scored. In a passionate and declamatory style the soloist enters with a dramatic version of Ex. 132. It isn't long before the rhythm of the third bar is condensed,

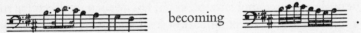

The quickening pulse of the music prompts a brief cadenza from the soloist into which Dvořák interpolates fanfare-like figures that are skilfully scored for woodwind rather than brass so as not to imperil the balance. Some climbing trills, against which flute and clarinet in turn continue to remind us of the important opening theme, lead to a gay and lively idea that might strike the uninitiated ear as something new. In fact it is a variation on Ex. 132, as this comparison plainly reveals; traces of the original pattern are still shown in Ex. 134[b].

Ex. 134

This episode has no counterpart in the orchestral exposition and is a delightful example of that element of fantasy that crops up so often in concertos. For some time the mood of frivolity continues until the 'cellist dramatically recalls the original shape and rhythm of Ex. 132. It is the last gesture of strength before the graceful descent to the second subject (Ex. 133) which the 'cello accepts gratefully, as well it might.

Now an essential aspect of a concerto is the display of virtuosity; there must of course be musical interest as well but a concerto that is just easy isn't really a concerto at all. While it is only too simple to write passages that *are* difficult for the 'cello it is a different matter to write ones that *sound* difficult. To be honest, the instrument lacks the facilities for display that the violin has; the sheer distance that the performer's hand has to cover presents one problem, while a string that is more than twice as long as a violin's cannot be expected to be as responsive in passages that demand rapid articulation. I say this not as a criticism of what is in fact my favourite string instrument, but rather in its defence, lest it should seem to be outshone by its more nimble sister. For instance, at the end of the second subject, Dvořák embarks on a long exploration of a tune whose salient feature is a rocking alternation of two adjacent notes; beneath it, the 'cello supplies a delicate and fluttering accompaniment.

Ex.135

There is a passage that is directly comparable to this in the Tschaikovsky violin concerto, beginning at bar 107 of the first movement. Quiet but sparkling triplets decorate a tune which again is mostly concerned with notes that are next-door neighbours but the difference in sheer brilliance is remarkable and can only be appreciated by the ear rather than the eye. It is in broad singing themes that the 'cello reaps an advantage, for in them its greater size is an asset and not a handicap.

Obviously Dvořák would have been very aware of this sort of problem, and it is interesting to look at the many revisions that he ultimately made to some of the more recalcitrant passages. Here are four different versions of bars 166-167. The first one is unenterprising and conventional and it is no surprise that he wanted to improve on it; the second is more difficult but not all that effective; the third is the suggestion of the 'cellist Wihan. Doubtless it lies well under the fingers, but it is a little turgid in texture. Dvořák's final choice is not only musically more interesting than the other three but is the most lyrical. His decision seems to have been governed then by a consideration of the specific virtues of the 'cello more than by anything else.

Ex. 136

The development proper begins with a longish orchestral section in which Ex. 132 goes through a number of transformations, moving to increasingly remote keys. There are moments of great beauty here, especially when Dvořák first begins to feel his way towards the unexpected tonality of A♭ minor.

Ex. 137

These sighing phrases are interspersed with that same fanfare figure that was mentioned earlier; it is still scored for woodwind, although it is only fair to say that it has also appeared on the horns on a couple of occasions. At last the soloist makes his long-delayed re-entry, this time with a particularly expressive version of Ex. 132, whose note-values are now doubled:

♩. ♫ | ♩.   becomes   ♩. ♫♩

This lyrical episode, in which the solo 'cello and the first flute share the melodic interest above a discreetly shimmering accompaniment from the strings, leads to a change of tempo. The music becomes more animated, even though for the most part it remains quiet. For some time the themes lie entirely in the orchestra while the soloist is kept busy with one constantly reiterated figure. Suddenly an increase of tone leads us to a more dramatic passage, and with a great wash of sound the full orchestra overwhelms the soloist with a triumphant version of Ex. 133, now in B major.

It is at this point that Dvořák introduces a remarkable modification of conventional 'sonata' form. What it amounts to is a by-pass in which he finds his way round the normal recapitulation of the first subject group and drives straight on to the second subject. Here is a rudimentary plan of a sonata form movement, with Dvořák's short cut shown in dotted lines.

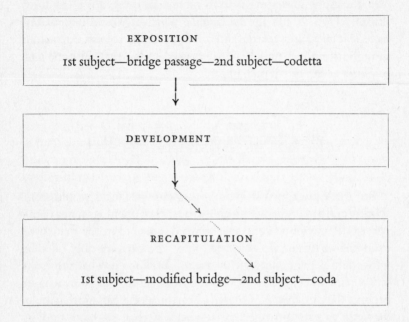

The final peroration is for the most part massively based on Ex. 132, and the movement comes to a magnificent conclusion without recourse to a cadenza.

The slow movement is rich in melodies, having a number of tunes of various shapes and sizes. First to greet our ears is a simple and pastoral affair scored for the woodwind family.

Ex.138

Almost immediately this is echoed quite simply by the soloist. A second phrase now appears and it is a matter of personal taste whether you regard it as a new theme or an extension of the old.

What is more interesting than its mere classification is to see how skilfully Dvořák fills up the lacunae which it would undeniably have if it were not for the intervention of the soloist. Attractive though its outlines may be, there is no denying that this tune sags mightily at the end of each phrase.

Ex.139

But these pockets that in any other circumstances would seem shoddy craftsmanship are precisely the sort of openings that a composer will leave in a concerto, as we discovered in the first three examples of this book. Needless to say, the gaps are duly filled in with some elegant phrases from the soloist. For a few bars, the solo 'cello part serves a purely decorative purpose, but soon it is to become the principal mourner in a heartbreaking passage that looks forward to the introspective meditation that we also find so movingly in the Elgar violoncello concerto. It is a strangely emotional theme to find after so unsophisticated an opening.

Ex.140

The woodwind make a forlorn attempt to remind us of Ex. 138, but Dvořák's imagination has turned to darker things and a dramatic phrase from the full orchestra puts us firmly in G minor. As a foil to this, the soloist offers a sustained melody which is actually an exact quotation from one of Dvořák's four songs, Op. 82. The composer had just heard that his sister-in-law, a charming young actress called Josefina Kounicová, was seriously ill, and with this song he was obviously expressing a nostalgic longing for his homeland. (There is a further quotation from Op. 82 in bars 468–473 of the finale of this concerto.) The movement alternates between the lyrical and the passionate, a series of falling semitones being a particularly beautiful example of musical lamentation. Towards the end there is a fascinating accompanied cadenza in which, within the limitations of his idiom, Dvořák anticipates an idea that we tend nowadays to regard as an invention of Bartók— or perhaps even Messiaen, since it is birds rather than insects that we hear. Above the broad elegiac phrases of the 'cello, a flute warbles like any thrush while bassoons croak like bullfrogs. It is a sudden evocation of the countryside in which we can detect Dvořák's dissatisfaction with the New York setting in which he found himself. As such, it is directly comparable to the second movement of Bartók's third piano concerto which, like this work, was written far from home. The final pages do, however, return to G major and the pastoral mood of the opening.

The finale starts as a march, somewhat *alla* Tschaikovsky. Over the distant tread of 'cellos and basses, the horns present us with a sketch of the main theme, a sketch since it lacks some important details which are kept back for the soloist to reveal. Here is the final version:

Ex. 141

The orchestra confirms this with due ceremony and then we begin a journey that takes us from one melody to another. It would be laborious to list them all here as subsidiary theme A, B, C and so on, since this would merely create complexity where in fact all is crystal clear. The music may not always comply with the pro- prieties of academic theory, but since it is utterly delightful to listen to why should we worry? Dvořák by now had his honorary

Doctorate (in Philosophy incidentally, but no matter) so he
scarcely needed to supply proof of his ability to comply with the
conventions. In fact the movement is a perfectly acceptable Rondo;
it is merely rather more richly endowed with themes than most. I
have counted no less than ten melodies which could be quoted as
having some importance, but several of them appear only once and
are then discarded.

A change of tempo in the middle of the movement leads to one
especially charming episode. As is so often the case in Dvořák's
music, the melody seems to be a genuine folk-song.

Ex. 142
Moderato

But this is soon displaced by a cocky little tune on the flute
against which the soloist practises his finger exercises in vain. There
are perhaps more passages of sheer virtuosity in this movement
than in its two predecessors, but Dvořák's natural fertility of
invention ensures that we are never bored. Towards the end the
music unwinds into an easy-paced Andante as muted trumpets
give out a gentle version of Ex. 141; it evokes a truly romantic
atmosphere—the golden glint of an evening sun touching a metal
breast plate against a darkly wooded background. Clarinets remind
us of the opening theme from the first movement, a recollection
which is taken up in turn by a solo horn and then by the first
violins. At last, with a great convulsion as though some giant wave
were gathering itself to beat against the shore, the music builds to a
tremendous climax. We prepare for a noble apotheosis, when
'Let's not take it too seriously', says Dvořák, and mischievously he
caps the movement with a delightfully flippant ending.

There had been earlier 'cello concertos than this but nevertheless
the Dvořák concerto must be accounted a notable step forward in
the genre; it will remain a firm favourite with 'cellists and audiences
alike as long as we continue to value emotional intensity, melodic
inspiration and rich colouring. These it has in abundance.

CHAPTER XI

RACHMANINOFF

Piano Concerto No. 3 in D minor, Op. 30 (1909)

1. Allegro ma non tanto. 2. Intermezzo: Adagio leading to poco piu mosso. 3. Finale: Alla breve.

Orchestra: 2 flutes; 2 oboes; 2 clarinets; 2 bassoons; 4 horns; 2 trumpets; 3 trombones; 1 tuba; timpani; percussion; strings.

CRITICAL ATTITUDES towards the music of Rachmaninoff are seldom wholly favourable. His music has been variously described as decadent, syrupy, diffuse, or garish; even in the supposedly unprejudiced pages of Grove's Dictionary we find mention of 'artificial and gushing tunes', 'an enormous popular success that is not likely to last', and other equally patronizing remarks. Yet to the despair of the critics, audiences continue to love this music while pianists still enjoy the challenge that it represents. It is so wonderfully written 'on the hands' that it gives an extraordinary physical pleasure to train the fingers to overcome the phenomenal difficulties. The third concerto is often summarily dismissed as a re-hash of the second; there are certainly resemblances of style between the two works, as there are between the first and second concertos of Beethoven for that matter. Both are constructed with an ingenuity that is masterly, and in the development of his material Rachmaninoff shows a far greater technical skill than we would imagine if we were to base our judgement solely on critical opinion. In this chapter I hope to show both the strengths and weaknesses of this work.

Two bars of softly murmuring accompaniment introduce the long first subject, a characteristic melody that is shaped very much as though it were a Russian folk-tune. The accompanying pattern, based as it is on the notes D F E, even suggests the outline of the melody to us before we actually hear it.

Ex. 143

It is essential that we should store this in our memory, long though it be, for the first movement is as much a set of variations on this theme as it is an example of normal concerto form. Once the pianist has disclosed the full twenty-four bars of the melody, the orchestra takes it over more or less intact, the soloist meanwhile decorating it with a striking pattern of quick-moving notes that has the purity of a Bach toccata. The writing becomes increasingly complex as, with quickening tempo, notes pour from the keyboard in a seemingly continuous flood. A quiet but important fanfare now catches our attention, first on horn and clarinet, then more clearly on trumpet and oboe.

Ex. 144

The orchestra settles into a soft chord of A major, the so-called 'dominant' of D minor, and a brief cadenza at last calls a halt to the rapid flow of notes that has streamed from the piano. In dark tones the 'cellos and basses recall the shape of the first few bars of Ex. 143 before a sudden surge of warm and voluptuous harmony suggests the imminent appearance of the second subject. Rachmaninoff's

craftsmanship here is notable. Ex. 144 has planted a rhythmic seed
in our minds; the strings now present us with a crisp and precise
little march rather than the languorous melody which the preceding bars have prepared us for. Its relationship to Ex. 144 is clear
enough.

Ex. 145

Within a matter of seconds the dry rhythms of Ex. 145a have
been translated into the lyrical expressiveness of Ex. 145b, and
what had seemed to be no more than an episode is revealed as the
foundation of the true second subject.

If to be original is to forge a style that is instantly recognizable
as one's own then Rachmaninoff is an original composer, for no
other hand could have penned this next passage. Perhaps it is over-
ripe, perhaps to some tastes it may seem altogether too lush, and
yet of its romantic type it is a notably successful example. We tend
to forget that it was written in 1909 not 1929; World War I had not
yet left its mark of toughness and cynicism on the face of European
art.

A quickening of pace and a flash of quicksilver from the keyboard bring us to an extension of Ex. 145b that is frequently cut in
performance.[1] This dissolves into a few glittering passages that
dart around a brief snatch of melody on the clarinet; the music
settles down quietly into D minor once again and the development
begins. Rachmaninoff first reminds us of Ex. 143; with a touch of
real magic he changes one note in the tune—the C sharp in bar 4
becomes a C natural. The resulting modulation into C major is
one of those moments that stays in the memory long after a
performance, so simple and yet so effective does it prove to be.

[1] I have only once heard a performance of this concerto without any cuts at all
(Van Cliburn's).

At first glance most of the material that now appears seems to be new and even irrelevant. In fact it is all closely connected to the first theme. What Rachmaninoff does is to select small fragments, groups of three notes or so, from Ex. 143 and build them into sequences. The following example should make the process easy to follow.

Ex. 146

These two derivations (146 a and b) are closely interlocked in a long and fascinating episode before the pianist embarks on a new figure of great complexity. This shows an even more ingenious variant on Ex. 143—which is here transposed into A minor so that the relationship is easier to follow.

Ex. 147

Time after time this pattern unfolds until the music spills over into a great climax of stamping chords which consist of a further extension of Ex. 146b. A battle royal develops between soloist and orchestra, a battle which resolves itself into a strangely bleak passage in which wisps of counterpoint float above lamenting semitones. Divided strings play some chords that have a curiously gasping effect; the cadenza begins.

This too is a set of skilful variations on Ex. 143. To begin with, the theme is there by implication even although it isn't actually stated; two bars should be enough to show Rachmaninoff's intentions.

Ex.148

This figure persists for some twenty-four bars of brilliantly
conceived piano writing; suddenly the pulse of the music changes
and a more immediately recognizable variant of Ex. 143 appears,
the hands playing alternate pairs of two-note chords that have the
curious effect of breaking the tune into fragments. The music
builds once more to a climax that gives dramatic evidence of
Rachmaninoff's formidable technique, especially in the rapid
playing of big chords, until a series of D major arpeggios brings us
to one of the most original passages in the whole concerto. The
cadenza seemingly continues in silvery ripples of notes that
gradually descend into a lower register, but against this harp-like
background other instruments gently join in to share the soloist's
limelight. Flute, oboe, clarinet and then horn in turn each play a
derivative of Ex. 143. In a typically rich cadence the piano part
resolves into the key of E flat major and we hear (for the first time
in the cadenza) a reference to Ex. 145b.

The cadenza says so much that Rachmaninoff feels no need for
any great extension afterwards. The coda is brief and to the point,
consisting of a reprise of Ex. 143 followed by no fewer than ten
references to Ex. 145a, above which the pianist indulges in some
glittering *chinoiserie* that makes an admirable warming-up
exercise for aspiring performers. The movement ends as quietly as
it had begun.

In the first movement we have encountered some clearly defined musical ideas which have already been developed with great ingenuity. In the remaining two movements we shall meet them again, for the concerto is conceived as one organic whole. Perhaps this is the moment to consider the enigma of Rachmaninoff's music. Why is it that critics tend to adopt so patronizing an attitude towards it? Is it just because by the hazards of their profession they hear too many performances of the piano concertos? In fact there are sound technical reasons for criticizing Rachmaninoff's composition at times; he has a tendency to 'sit down' too often and too obviously in long-drawn-out cadences that are far too self-indulgent. His themes depend overmuch on a step-by-step progress that makes them little more than disguised scales. The texture of the music is often too rich, and any pianist who has worked at this third concerto will say 'Too many notes' with considerable emphasis. One other fault we shall consider in detail in analysing the last movement. Now these criticisms are perfectly valid, but against them we must weigh other equally important considerations. I have already suggested that we tend to be a little confused in our placing of these works historically. Because Rachmaninoff was so dominant and memorable a personality on the concert platform right up to the nineteen-forties we forget that the second concerto was written as long ago as 1901. I suspect that if one took into consideration every composition written between the years 1900 and 1909 it would be impossible to find two major works that have been so frequently performed as the second and third concertos of Rachmaninoff. How then have they survived when a critical ear can so easily discern weaknesses of one kind or another?

There is in most of us a sybaritic streak that revels in soft cushions, luxurious beds, perfume and sweetmeats. The voluptuous, opulent quality of Rachmaninoff's music appeals to this side of our natures. Maybe Czarist Russia was a decadent state, founded on corruption, injustice and cruelty; but for the nobility it was a world in which beauty and sensibility were highly valued, if in a somewhat self-indulgent way. Something of this is reflected in this music, and we may enjoy it in much the same way as we might enjoy a good film about Russia at the turn of the century. The actual construction of the music is often remarkably ingenious, and it is a serious error to dismiss these concertos as mere claptrap. In the long run it comes to a simple matter of taste, by which I mean not that bane of our times, 'Good Taste', but personal preference. The diet may be too rich for some stomachs, but if some of us do not care for peach melba we still have no right to condemn it as a dish. One must accept, however, that Rachmaninoff cannot make a dish that will suit all tables, as Beethoven or Mozart can.

The slow movement begins with a long orchestral introduction that is not by any means the finest page in the concerto—here are those self-same repetitive cadences of which one can legitimately complain. The orchestration is beautiful but the content is too dependent on drooping phrases that get nowhere. But once the piano enters there are some marvellously conceived passages for keyboard; in particular, the conflicting rhythms of three against five, five against eight and so forth, are wonderfully effective in conveying an impression of spontaneity. In due course the pianist reveals the full span of the melody at which the orchestra has been hinting for some time. It begins and ends in D flat major and its adherence to that key is confirmed by no less than six cadences. This again must be counted a weakness in construction, for the ear must tire of being told the same thing over and over again. Yet these cadences are a hallmark of Rachmaninoff's style and we must accept them as such unless we are prepared to lose the good things as well.

The writing for the piano grows increasingly rhapsodic until at one point (again omitted in most performances) the first violins reintroduce Ex. 143 from the first movement. The reason for the cut is tragically obvious when we realize that the root of the harmony here remains firmly on F for eighteen bars; the richness of the decoration that floods from the keyboard cannot disguise the poverty of the bass that underlies it. It was Stanford who used to cover the upper parts of a pupil's composition and expose the bass in all its naked inadequacy, and one cannot help feeling that in this one respect Rachmaninoff might have taken a useful lesson. There follows, as if by some law of natural compensation, one of his finest climaxes; three rising waves of melody in the piano part gather their strength slowly, to break in a great wash of sound in the remote key of D major before a skilful change of harmonic direction brings us back to D flat again and an even more exultant version of the main theme of the movement.

The mood suddenly changes as mercurial triplets dance from the pianist's fingers. A scherzo is ingeniously fitted into the middle of the slow movement. The strings begin a quick waltz accompaniment, while beneath the glittering figuration from the piano, clarinet and bassoon play a delicately syncopated tune.

Ex.149

etc.

Closer inspection shows this to be Ex. 143 wearing fancy dress; rhythm and pitch have changed but the contours remain the same.

Ex.150

etc.

Play Ex. 150 on the piano and it will sound a somewhat distorted version of the theme from the first movement, for as a further disguise Rachmaninoff has moved the tune up a note in the scale, as though one were to play the National Anthem like this:

Ex.151

No explanation or analysis can diminish the ingenuity of this passage, which introduces variety by its change of mood and tempo, but which also serves to cement the two movements more firmly together. Rachmaninoff even throws in a few fleeting references to the original form of Ex. 143 in the pianist's left hand just to show willing. They are seldom appreciated by an audience, but they are there for his own satisfaction.

Ex. 152

The fireworks splutter and die, the orchestra resumes the initial mood of the movement. We seem about to embark on a lengthy recapitulation when some abrupt octaves from the piano cut sharply into the prevailing melancholy. With a whoosh and a roar we are launched into the finale.

This begins with a strong rhythmic background in the woodwind against which the pianist discharges a fanfare-like figure that periodically spills over into handfuls of chromatic notes. After some thirty-eight bars of this, a splendid new theme appears.

Ex. 153

Exciting though this is, it is no more than an interlude; indeed it is difficult to decide precisely what form this movement belongs to, since it is neither a rondo nor a sonata-form movement. A series of themes appears one after the other, each one being destined to return at least once later in the proceedings, sometimes in a rather different guise. Of these two more must be quoted. The first begins with three repeated minim chords before getting under way, but these do not appear in the example.

Ex.154

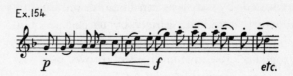

The syncopations are heavily underlined by stamping chords in both hands, the left hand giving an athletic character to the phrase by means of some awkward leaps down to the low C which is the harmonic foundation of the whole theme. As a foil to this we find a more lyrical tune which however shares something of the same contour in its rise and fall.

Ex.155

Climbing ever higher in mounting sequences, this melody has the true Rachmaninoff touch, and despite a plethora of notes in the keyboard part is marvellously scored. A continuation of the urgent syncopations from Ex. 154 lies beneath it, effectively preventing sentiment from getting too much of an upper hand. The opening rhythms return in a brief outburst from the orchestra; the marching phrases grow quieter, and in a rather too obvious cadence the music settles a little ponderously on to the chord of E flat major. We have arrived at an extreme example of Rachmaninoff's ingenuity and ineptitude; seldom can any composer have shown the two characteristics in such equal measure at one time. The ineptitude lies in the orchestral part which stays firmly rooted on an E flat bass for what seems like an eternity—in fact it is virtually thirty-three bars of slow four or six. There are a couple of minor diversions but they quickly return to base. The ingenuity, which I freely confess is much more evident in performance, consists of a fascinating piano part in which Ex. 145^b from the first movement reappears in an enchantingly capricious guise. Ex. 156 shows the two versions side by side, the second one being simplified a little in its notation so that the comparison is clearer.

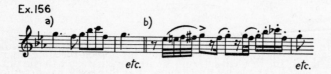

Above the luxurious cushion of harmony provided by the strings, the piano part swoops and darts in little scurries of notes; it is a wonderfully imagined bit of keyboard writing, only spoilt by this regrettable inability to escape from the deadening continuity of E flat that lies beneath. Ex. 156ᵇ is developed still further against a background of watery runs of great delicacy before we settle down once more on to a firm cadence of E♭ major.

The following section, a more rhapsodic treatment of Ex. 156ᵇ, is usually cut since it too finds it difficult to break away from the E flat bass. Suddenly a familiar theme appears as violas and 'cellos reintroduce a brooding version of Ex. 143, the very first theme of the concerto. This kindles nostalgic memories in the pianist, and the expressive second subject (Ex. 145ᵇ) duly appears in the welcome tonality of E major, the first significant departure from E flat for a very long time. The music accumulates into an impassioned climax which disintegrates into one last mercurial section of quicksilver writing for the keyboard.

A sort of recapitulation follows in which we meet all the themes of the finale once more. The order of events remains unchanged, though needless to say some details are different. A simpler treatment of Ex. 155 is even more effective; but its lyrical outpouring is suddenly halted by a series of abrupt disjointed phrases that sound remarkably like the noises made by a departing train. These are immensely exciting but seem to be irrelevant. Actually they represent the most cunning join of all from first to third movements, for it is the cadenza which now reappears. A comparison of the following chord sequence with Ex. 148 will prove instructive.

Ex.157

etc.

Rachmaninoff gains little credit for so masterly a feat as the average critic is so busy looking down his nose at the tunes that he fails to notice the clever bits. I hope that this essay has given due weight to the composer's virtues while admitting his weaknesses.

The movement ends with an apotheosis of Ex. 154, its syncopations now removed, and the whole arch of melody smoothed out in such a way as to suggest a marriage between it and Ex. 155. A last torrent of octaves and chords causes the audience to give an ovation to the pianist—for this concerto is one of the most formidable challenges in the entire repertoire. Uneven it may be, diffuse and over-full of notes, but its virtues remain evident and its appeal enormous. Not even its most disparaging critic can deny that the imprint of the composer's personality is clear in every bar.

CHAPTER XII

BARTÓK

Concerto for Orchestra (1943)

1. Introduzione. 2. Giuoco delle coppie (Game with pairs). 3. Elegia.
4. Intermezzo interrotto. 5. Finale.

Orchestra: 3 flutes; 3 oboes (3rd doubling cor anglais); 3 clarinets
(3rd doubling bass clarinet); 3 bassoons (3rd doubling double
bassoon); 4 horns; 3 trumpets—4 if available; 2 tenor trombones;
1 bass trombone; tuba; timpani; 2 percussion players; 2 harps;
strings.

TO INCLUDE a concerto for orchestra in this volume may seem
a little perverse; is its title not a mere play on words, giving a
scanty disguise to a symphony? Not at all. As has been shown
already in the first chapter, the earliest concertos were works in
which the best players of a group were given more elaborate
passages to play than those allotted to their neighbours. Bartók's
logical conclusion was that since the orchestra in the twentieth
century had become a virtuoso instrument in its own right it was
only fair that it should be given a piece designed specifically to
reveal that virtuosity. In the event he produced a masterpiece that is
far more than a vehicle for display, for it is its imaginative quality
that makes the most enduring impression. Before we explore it in
detail let us briefly consider Bartók's music.

What is music? A fair definition would be to describe it as 'the
organization of sounds in patterns of melody and harmony'; but
who is to judge what is melody or harmony? When someone
observes that such-and-such a modern composer's music shows
absolutely no knowledge of harmony the chances are that he really

means that his own knowledge of harmony is not nearly so advanced as the composer's. Frederick Corder, who was a distinguished musician in his own right, once said of Bartók's music,

> If you were so rash as to purchase any of Béla Bartók's compositions, you would find that they each and all consist of unmeaning bunches of notes, apparently representing the composer promenading the keyboard in his boots. Some can be played better with the elbows, others with the flat of the hand. None require fingers to perform nor ears to listen to.[1]

Strong stuff, and it leaves no loopholes; 'they *each and all* consist of unmeaning bunches of notes'. Does that include this?[2]

Ex. 158
Andante

I would like to have heard Mr Corder playing that with his elbows—they would have had to be a little more discriminating than most people's.

Now it would be foolish to deny that some (or even much) of Bartók's music is difficult to the uninitiated ear. He is a composer who had to contend with ignorant hostility all his life, a composer whose music makes no particular attempt to court popular favour, but who persisted on his lonely way despite poverty, persecution and ridicule. It is the classic situation once again, the great composer who only finds real acceptance after his death. But that acceptance

---

[1] *Musical Quarterly*, New York, July 1915.
[2] No. 1 of *Three Rondos on Folk Tunes* (Boosey and Hawkes).

has surely come, and professional musicians the world over are now in agreement as to his qualities.

The best way to approach the concerto for orchestra is through the imagination. The mere fact that it has five movements, some of which have titles, should make us realize that its formal plan is at the least unusual. Much of the music is extraordinarily evocative, suggesting visual images as powerfully as the most accomplished film score. One important aspect of Bartók's music that we should never forget, though, is his very different musical background. We do not have to have learned a great deal about European history to know that the Turks at one time penetrated far into the centre of Europe. As a souvenir of their passage they left behind a wholly different musical culture which imbued central European folk-music with rhythms and intervals that are quite unlike those that we normally regard as Western. There are two exotic elements in European folk-song—the strong Moorish influence that still exists in Spanish flamenco singing, and the Turkish influence in the music of Hungary and Rumania. This is reflected in Bartók, who like Vaughan Williams assimilated his native folk-song into his own music; but to expect him to *sound* like Vaughan Williams or Elgar would be as futile as to imagine that one could make a distinguished-looking foreigner look like an Englishman simply by dressing him in Savile Row. Bartók *is* foreign to English ears and we must accept that fact. However, he has a great deal to say that is worthy of our attention; what we need is a phrase-book, and a willingness to accommodate ourselves to the flavour of his cooking. This concerto makes an admirable introduction to his music; it has comedy, drama and pathos; it shows off a galaxy of orchestral colours with the utmost brilliance. As for the snobbish element who tend to look down on it as 'pop' Bartók, I have little patience with them; with their inflated intellects they ought to know better.

The work begins in utter darkness; occasionally a pair of flutes suggest some nocturnal sound—the hoot of an owl perhaps. 'Cellos and basses begin by establishing the enormously important interval of a fourth.

Ex. 159
Andante non troppo

A factual description of the first twenty bars or so would tell us that it begins with unison 'cellos and basses playing a slow theme, followed by a quiet rustling figure on the upper strings with fragments of melody on the woodwind—a description that fits the start of Schubert's Unfinished symphony equally well. Since the two works are palpably different it is worth our while to consider why. There is a difference of purpose as much as of idiom. Schubert is concerned with themes; admittedly he presents them in arresting colours, but they are designed to be memorable and to establish a tonality which is the home-key of B minor. Bartók's music reflects the complete change that has come over twentieth-century music. His themes are what one might call anti-themes, shapes rather than melodies, shapes which are purposely left vague and nebulous. The first phrase has a twofold purpose; emotionally it suggests darkness and brooding melancholy; intellectually it tells us to think of fourths. The rustle on the violins is nothing more than a haze—atmospheric colouring of no thematic importance. Nor is it over-fanciful to suggest that the trill on the flutes is a bird-call; Bartók was a great nature-lover, and we often hear the sounds of birds and insects in his works. Gradually out of this featureless dark there begin to emerge suggestions of melody. A few notes, a stop, a few notes, another stop—groping forward while the early morning mist swirls around in giant coils, making a tree loom suddenly large, a bush seem like a crouching panther. The fourths of Ex. 159 become a continuous flow of quavers while trumpets reiterate a brief pattern of notes from which the main theme, once it arrives, really stems. At last the tune is grasped firmly; it is a passionate melody, even although its intervals may seem a little strange. Its sinuous curves suggest the lithe movements of a dancer.

Ex.160

This romantic outburst finally dispels the morning mist, and
with increasing enthusiasm Bartók seizes on one small fragment of
music, five rising notes[1] that have served as a background to the
last phrases (not quoted here) of the melody above. The pattern is
repeated obsessionally through a steady increase of pace; suddenly
they explode into a new and important theme that combines the
idea of fourths with that of the five rising notes.

Ex.161
Allegro vivace

It is Bartók's pleasure to split this theme up, and a long development section now ensues in which he explores every possibility
contained within the two sections marked 1 and 2. He also introduces another idea that goes hand in hand with the elaborate and
dexterous treatment of these two fragments. Again it is based on
the ubiquitous fourths.

Ex.162

One of the most splendid passages in the whole work is a fugal
section based on Ex. 162 and scored for the full brass, punctuated

[1] Fig. 1 in Ex. 161, but their initial appearance is at a much slower tempo.

by athletic outbursts of Ex. 161 on wind or strings. Another important but much less aggressive phrase oscillates gently between two adjacent notes in a rhythm which certainly has a relationship to Ex. 161, fig. 2. These quotations are little more than a phrase-book, however, and it is better in the initial stages to surrender to the power and colour of the music rather than to bother overmuch with the why and wherefore. Perhaps the best explanation of Bartók's technique is to see it as a variation on a stock classical procedure; whereas Brahms or Beethoven will develop a theme, shortening it, lengthening it, turning it upside down, extending its rhythm and so on,[1] Bartók will take a simple musical concept such as a fourth or five running notes. From this elementary idea he will produce a family of themes which are inter-related because they all have a fourth in them, just as even remote cousins might all share blue eyes, fair hair, or a bulbous nose.

The second movement is founded on a similar conception. It is called 'Giuoco delle Coppie', or 'game with pairs'. Its unity is derived not so much from the development of themes as from the idea of pairs of wind instruments. After a brief and arresting drum rhythm, we begin with a pair of bassoons. For a little time they disport themselves like a couple of porpoises, while accompanying strings snap out the rhythm beneath. Then we have two oboes; it is an entirely different tune that they play, but somehow the similarity of layout is enough to make it seem a perfectly logical continuation. So it goes on, with a pair of clarinets, a pair of flutes and a pair of trumpets.[2] Each couple brings its own contribution to this musical Noah's Ark while the accompaniment grows increasingly complex. The shimmering fluttering background that the strings

[1] See Chapter I of *Talking about Symphonies* for a discussion of classical development sections.

[2] It is worth mentioning that each pair of instruments adheres to one type of interval; thus we have successive sections in which we find parallel sixths, thirds, sevenths, fifths and seconds. The final sustained chord compresses all these into a single harmony before the concluding solo drum ends the movement.

provide for the trumpets is a particularly fascinating example of Bartók's virtuosity as an orchestrator.

In the middle of the movement there is a strange little chorale for brass; only a quiet side-drum reminds us of the rhythmic excitement of the first part. Then oboe, flute, and clarinet in turn try to launch the original bassoon theme once more. It is a delicate and enchanting moment, as though they can't quite remember how it went. The bassoons pick it up, this time *à trois*, and the games begin again. The texture is thicker as now the pairs begin to play together, but just as we are expecting a noisy ending Bartók closes the lid and the movement ends as it had begun with a single side-drum.

The central elegy is an extraordinary piece, full of strange noises that ripple through the woodwind. Debussy would have recognized it as a logical extension of his impressionism. It begins with the same crepuscular shadows that we found at the start of the first movement, and then the underwater ripples begin. It is impossible to say if it is Bartók's intention to illustrate the plash and gurgle of tiny fountains or whether he is merely doodling with sound. The effect is hypnotic and magical.

Suddenly a piercing high D flat on oboe and clarinet freezes all movement. The whole texture changes to a complicated net of arch-like phrases out of which emerges the very figure that the trumpets had originally toyed with in the first movement (see p. 138). In bold strokes Bartók outlines a dramatic development of this fragmentary theme. Mysterious and ghostly noises suggest imaginary terrors before Ex. 160 reappears convulsed in torment. A great wailing climax dissolves into falling fourths, only to be submerged once more beneath the watery cascades of clarinets and flutes. The movement has no story but it speaks to us in terms of a child's picture-book. Here is a castle, there a wood, there a strange underwater kingdom of mermaids and enchanted princesses locked in a cave of eternal ice. It is fatal to listen to this music in terms of the classical composer, or to try to relate it to the familiar world of the symphonic repertoire. It is full of imagination and colour; read into it what you like.

The fourth movement, an 'interrupted intermezzo', has become positively popular, with its attractive folk-melody and the irreverent lampoon of Shostakovich in the middle. The initial theme on the oboe has a haunting lilt to it.

Ex.163
Allegretto

This is developed in several ways, of which the most characteristic is to fit it against its own reflection, mirror-like. The mood is gentle and unassuming, with the strings holding sustained harmonies in the background. The first time their presence is really felt is with a voluptuous tune on the violas accompanied by declamatory chords on the harp. First violins and cor anglais together show their approval of this memorable tune before Ex. 163 returns once more in its original almost plaintive guise.

Delicately at first, but then with increasing abandon a vamping rhythm appears in the strings. Above it, a solo clarinet introduces a tune composed entirely of descending sequences.

Ex.164

It seems that, while working on this concerto, Bartók heard Shostakovich's seventh symphony ('The Leningrad') for the first time. He thought the all-pervading theme of the march absurd and decided to caricature it in his own work. Here it is, and the Rabelaisian raspberry with which it is greeted makes Bartók's opinion abundantly clear. Each attempt to restart the Shostakovich theme is greeted with a gust of laughter from the orchestra. Sanity is restored with the dignified and noble tune which the violas had originally presented; Ex. 163 is turned upside down once again, but in the gentlest possible way; the movement ends with three clear chords of B major that might have brought some small comfort to Mr Frederick Corder's tormented soul.

The finale delights in the virile dance-rhythms that are to be found so frequently in Bartók's music. A brief fanfare on the horns and we are away, lower strings thrumming and twanging while the violins scurry through a study in perpetual motion. It is scarcely worth quoting in print since the eye is hard put to it to keep up with the sounds here. Some contrast is provided by occasional patches in a varied rhythm,

Ex. 165

but this is not as important as might be supposed. The mad whirl continues with wisps of melody flying past as though seen from a train window; all are too insubstantial to grasp. Suddenly a single bassoon finds that he has the field to himself; bravely he begins a fugal subject in which his fellow wind-players soon become involved.

Ex. 166

A romantic flute turns the phrase the other way up, playing capricious tricks with its rhythm and making it seem almost seductive. For a time, something of the elemental energy of the movement disappears, but it isn't long before the wild activity begins again. As though everything up to this point had been a series of sketches, Bartók now introduces the real meat of the movement—one of the most elaborate fugues that he ever wrote.

Ex.167

To preserve its vitality a form must be adaptable, and when I describe this as a fugue you must not expect it to adhere strictly to the classical pattern. For one thing the subject appears not in isolation but surrounded by the furious hubbub of the full orchestra; for another it is immediately inverted, a procedure which would undoubtedly have caused Bartók to fail any diploma examination. But here is the whole concept of fugue seen through twentieth-century eyes. Every academic trick is imposed upon the material; it is played in notes of double the value, of half the value, it is inverted, it is treated in stretto (i.e. with overlapping entries). New ingenuities abound, developments of the subject which shed a further light on its character. It is as though the notes were made of some flexible substance that enable them to be stretched and moulded in an infinite variety of ways without ever losing some element of their original shape. Perhaps the most enduring impression of the movement lies in its demonic energy. Even when the fugue subject appears in a last augmentation it is shot through with hurricane scales in strings and wind. The furious pace of the music reflects something of the creative fever that Bartók must have experienced to write such a piece in the incredibly brief period of seven weeks.

Our acceptance of Bartók is now becoming more than lip-service, and he is no longer the bogey-man that he once seemed to be. What a fine and passionate spirit was his; how honest his beliefs, how uncompromising his utterance, how penetrating his ear that could seek out and find such beauty in the strange crannies of music.

INDEX